Praise for *How to Close a Deal Like Warren Buffett*

"When you walk through the Omaha airport, there is a picture of Warren Buffett's graduating class from the University of Nebraska and his quote, "Invest in yourself." Once you understand that there is an art and a science to making the deal, you'll understand the value of Warren Buffett's quote. Investing in yourself is not an option; it's an imperative, and investing in this book is exactly the same. Getting the wisdom and thinking behind Warren Buffett's deals will help you gain insight into the art and science of making your deals."

—Jeffrey Gitomer, author of *The Little Red Book of Selling*

"Tom Searcy and Henry DeVries uncover Warren Buffett's secrets to closing the biggest deals in the world. They'll teach you the skills to make your first million dollar deal."

—Dan Waldschmidt, author of *Edgy Conversations*

"Tom Searcy and Henry DeVries have done a masterful job of distilling Buffett's wisdom into a highly readable book you'll want to refer to again and again. A must-have for dealmakers!"

—Ken Blanchard, coauthor of *The One Minute Manager*®
and *Leading at a Higher Level*

"Almost anybody interested in deal making, from salespeople to CEOs, will find something of interest here. Simply the most important new book on deal making and big account sales strategy."

—Marshall Goldsmith, million-selling author or editor of
32 books, including the *New York Times* bestsellers *MOJO*
and *What Got You Here Won't Get You There*

"Read this inspiring, advice-filled book to discover how you can leverage Warren Buffett's deal-making strategies to negotiate and win big contracts."

—Jill Konrath, author of *SNAP Selling* and *Selling to Big Companies*

How to Close a Deal Like

WARREN BUFFETT

Lessons from the World's Greatest Dealmaker

TOM SEARCY AND HENRY DEVRIES

New York   Chicago   San Francisco   Lisbon   London   Madrid   Mexico City
Milan   New Delhi   San Juan   Seoul   Singapore   Sydney   Toronto

1 2 3 4 5 6 7 8 9 0 DOC/DOC 1 8 7 6 5 4 3 2

ISBN: 978-0-07-180165-2
MHID: 0-07-180165-0

e-book ISBN: 978-0-07-180166-9
e-book MHID: 0-07-180166-9

Interior design by Monica Baziuk

McGraw-Hill books are available at special quantity discounts to use as premiums and sales promotions, or for use in corporate training programs. To contact a representative please e-mail us at bulksales@mcgraw-hill.com.

This book is printed on acid-free paper.

To our inspiration, Warren Buffett and Charlie Munger.

Studying them, Berkshire Hathaway, and its managers

has been a pleasure and a gift to us

Contents

ACKNOWLEDGMENTS

We wish to thank *CBS MoneyWatch* for believing in Tom as an online columnist. This is where the seed of the idea for *How to Make Deals Like Warren Buffett* sprouted in column form. We want to thank Donya Dickerson of McGraw-Hill, who persistently encouraged us to bring to readers the lessons of the greatest dealmaker in the world. We are grateful to friends and authors Robin Ryan and Dan Janal for their insights during the proposal process. Special thanks go to our researchers, Karla DeVries and Don Sevrens, for their assistance in gathering information. We also want to express our thanks to the Berkshire Hathaway managers who helped us with fact checking the manuscript. Perhaps the biggest thanks go to our team at Hunt Big Sales, especially our president, Carajane Moore, and the most valuable player, Jessie Kelley. Because we never wanted this book to be theory without practical applications, a nod of thanks also to the Hunt Big Sales clients that allowed their case studies to be included in the book to illustrate the Warren Buffett lessons. Tom would also like to thank his wife, Jen, and Henry his wife, Vikki, for their understanding of the lost nights and weekends during the research and writing of the book.

INTRODUCTION

You Aren't Warren, but You Can Make Deals Like Him

The Berkshire Hathaway (stock symbol BRK) annual shareholders' meeting in Omaha, Nebraska, is truly to capitalists what the Daytona 500 is to NASCAR fans. It's a spectacle, a tradition, and a happening. The event is over the top and reassuringly familiar to the faithful.

At this writing, a single share of BRK-A sells for more than $120,000, but a share of BRK-B is about $80. The good news is that either share will qualify you for a ticket to the annual meeting. It's worth the expense of buying either type of share and the travel and time required to attend this crash course in business excellence.

As part of our research for this book, my coauthor, Henry DeVries, and I attended the 2012 annual session in Omaha and got the chance to meet all sorts of great people, including the CEO of Dairy Queen, the founder of the Pampered Chef, the CEO of World Book, senior executives of Burlington Northern Santa Fe Railway, and many other leaders of the various companies owned by Berkshire Hathaway.

From meeting and watching these company CEOs and executives, we learned something about them that is also true of many of the successful business leaders that we have met over time, regardless of the size of their companies. Surprisingly, it's love.

1. *They love their customers.* Hollywood often portrays business leaders as stuffed suits, brusque and self-important. Not this group. They are on fire, accessible, warm, and friendly. They seek and serve their customers and shareholders with genuine interest. Warren (we will be on a first-name basis with him throughout the book) likes to tell shareholders that the managers who run the companies Berkshire owns are all rich enough to quit any day, but they stay for reasons other than money.

2. *They love what they sell.* I got the opportunity to talk to the founder of the Pampered Chef for a moment. She pulled me over to three different products that were on sale for half price, $5 each. I had the leader of a billion-dollar company demonstrating a no-drip wine stopper as if we were in my home and she'd brought it as a host gift. I got a Dilly Bar from Dairy Queen served with a smile and a "Still love 'em after all these years—they are just the best!" by the CEO of Dairy Queen. The excitement hasn't left these people, despite the millions they have earned or their international notoriety. They still love their products and services and can't wait to tell people about them.

3. *They love what they do.* Watching these people work the booth, talk to shareholders and customers, and chat with their staff, you would think you were attending an Up with People! rally. Working the floor is neither beneath them nor a burden. They love what they do, and they bring the energy to everything they are doing.

4. *They love their people.* Elbow to elbow with their frontline people, these people were not followed by an entourage. If their badges hadn't been a different color, you would have had some difficulty picking out the executives from the other members of the team. Joking while they were jostling in the crowd, setting the pace for reaching out to customers, and pitching in—it was clear to me that these leaders love their people.

Nobody believes that excellence like this just happens. There is, of course, a person who has been responsible for bringing these exemplary managers together, and that person is Warren.

What's the Big Deal About Buffett?

This book is not about *Warren the amazing investor*, by the numbers; that book has been written several times. This is about *Warren the dealmaker*, an inspiring and instructional take for the more than 50 million people in America who make their livelihood by negotiating and landing deals.

Warren might catch flack in some quarters, but if you want to know about closing big deals, he's still the guy to watch. Why? The man knows how to talk about money when he's making deals. What he has when he goes into any conversation is an encyclopedic knowledge of how businesses work financially. He knows "their money," "their wallet," and how investments and outcomes should work. Follow his lead and you will close more business.

"Risk," says Warren, "comes from not knowing what you are doing." For the most part, Warren did his homework, so he knew what he was doing. Here are just a few examples:

=== WARREN WAY 60 ===

Love Is the Greatest Return

From the Buffett biography *The Snowball*: "That's the ultimate test of how you have lived your life. The trouble with love is you can't buy it. You can buy sex. You can buy testimonial dinners. You can buy pamphlets that say how wonderful you are. But the only way to get love is to be lovable."

1. When he was 20, he invested more than half of his net worth in GEICO, an insurance company. By 1995, he had closed deals to own all of the company.
2. He was able to buy See's Candies for $25 million because he saw it as a high-quality company with growth potential.
3. In a 60-second negotiation, he agreed to a price of $100 million, 10 times annual earnings, for Central States Indemnity Company.
4. He paid $315 million for Scott Fetzer Companies, a conglomerate that includes the makers of Kirby vacuum cleaners and World Book Encyclopedia.

Other purchases of note have included Mars/William Wrigley Jr. Co., Fruit of the Loom, Garan children's clothing, CORT Business Services, Business Wire, Brooks Sports, Nebraska Furniture Mart, Borsheims, Helzberg Diamonds, RC Willey, Ben Bridge Jeweler, Justin Brands, NetJets, *Omaha World-Herald*, Burlington Northern Santa Fe Railway, Benjamin Moore & Co., and Clayton Homes. Some of these stories that best illustrate Warren's deal-making lessons are chronicled in this book.

Calling All Dealmakers

Don't assume that your deals don't compare to those in Warren's world. The targeted readers for this book are the more than 50 million business owners, entrepreneurs, sales professionals, and people in related occupations whose businesses live and die by getting money to flow toward the opportunities they represent. According to the 2010 U.S. Census, these include

1. The 22.6 million self-employed professionals, consultants, and business owners, who make deals to land clients and contracts
2. The 15.4 million sales professionals and people in related occupations (advertising salespeople, business development consultants, insurance agents, real estate brokers and agents, sales

reps, securities and financial services salespeople), who make deals to land accounts

3. The 5.8 million corporate CEOs, who are the chief dealmakers for their organizations

4. The 1 million business transaction attorneys, who close deals on behalf of clients and for themselves

5. The millions of business leaders who are equally interested in money flow and deal-making opportunities, including executives involved in corporate strategic planning

In addition, the book was also written for the more than 6 million entrepreneurs who create new businesses every year in America and the tens of thousands of people in the United States who are employed in venture capital firms, investment banks, business brokers, and other facets of the mergers and acquisitions industry.

For myself, I know that this works. As of this writing, my biggest Warren Buffett–type deal was a $400 million contract. Using the ideas that we are going to discuss, my companies and client companies have closed more than $5 billion in new business. These deals have ranged in size from $10,000 to more than $100,000,000. This approach has been used in financial services, manufacturing, construction, distribution, logistics, professional services, and many other industries. Everyone has the chance to change his vista by changing the types of deals he pitches and closes. To do it—to set the bar higher in your sales life—you must have a plan. That plan is what you'll find in the following pages.

Over the years, I have been very fortunate to work with many marvelous clients who have graciously allowed me to tell you about their experiences. Therefore, you'll find

= **WARREN WAY 90** =

Marry Your Fortunes Well

Buffett once said: "Our situation is the opposite of Camelot's Mordred, of whom Guenevere commented, 'The one thing I can say for him is that he is bound to marry well. Everybody is above him.'"

client stories interspersed throughout the book. I use these stories as examples, of course, but also as my tribute to the dedication and hard work exhibited by clients time and time again. They provide me with a large portion of my inspiration on a daily basis. And for that, I'm truly grateful.

For full disclosure, I am a stockholder in Warren Buffett's holding company, Berkshire Hathaway, and a faithful reader of the folksy and informative annual letter to shareholders that he began in 1970. Buffett has not commented on, endorsed, or sanctioned this manuscript.

Before I was 40, I had headed four corporations, each of which I took from annual revenues of less than $15 million to more than $100 million. Those were fantastic experiences for me, but I discovered along the way that what I really love doing is working with others to help them have the kind of experiences I had.

So I founded Hunt Big Sales, a fast-growth sales consultancy. Altogether, I have worked with more than 150 companies, helping them use the principles in this book to land multimillion-dollar key accounts.

My coauthor, Henry, is part of my Hunt Big Sales consulting team. He is also a marketing researcher and newspaper columnist who has spent the last three decades studying deal making. In addition, Henry serves on the marketing faculty and is the assistant dean of the continuing education division of the University of California–San Diego.

We owe a debt to our Hunt Big Sales team, especially our president, Carajane Moore, a dealmaker extraordinaire, and Wil Davis, a former CEO client who followed the system to double his company and is the current head of our HBS Academy, the place where companies that want to double in size go to learn how to close the deals that make it possible.

Throughout the book, we shall use the editorial we. Some of the examples are Tom's, and others are Henry's, some are Carajane's, some are Wil's, and so forth. For ease of reading, we have married the thoughts into one narrative.

Enough preamble; deal making waits for no one. Let's get started.

TOM SEARCY
Founder, Hunt Big Sales
May 2012

How to Close a Deal Like

WARREN
BUFFETT

The Quest to Make Deals Like Warren

O N ANY given day in Omaha, Nebraska, in 1983, it would not have been unusual to see Rose Blumkin, the 89-year-old founder and owner of the largest single furniture store company in America, driving her scooter around her mini-empire, Nebraska Furniture Mart. However, one day that year, some customers saw something that was unusual: she was in the middle of an aisle, negotiating with future billionaire Warren Buffett over the sale of her company.

"Warren," she said, "I'm tired of fighting with my children over how to run this place, and I want to slow down."

"Rose, I've always told you that when you were ready to sell, I would buy. What's your price?" replied Warren.

They shook hands, and the deal was done. He gave her a hand-written check for $55 million, and the Blumkin clan went into partnership with his company, Berkshire Hathaway.

Does that sound impulsive? Not Warren. He followed several of his key principles in making this deal:

1. Know your numbers, their numbers, and all the numbers of the industry.

2. Make deals with the kind of people you would like to be in business with.
3. When it's time to make the deal, don't blink.

Back in 1983, the family that had created one of the iconic brands in the furniture industry made a deal to join forces with the future wealthiest man in the world. The deal was done in the course of an hour with a handwritten check and without a single lawyer present. That deal has stood to this day and has greatly benefited both parties.

The Way to Your Warren Buffett Deal

Do you remember the biggest deal you ever made?

Of course you do. Everyone has one, and everyone remembers it. How could you forget? Many times, you've gone back over that deal in your mind. You have probably replayed the deal, reviewing what led to its success. You examined the tactic you used that worked perfectly—even though you were pretty sure it wouldn't. You remembered any cringe-inducing moments and swore that you'd never go through anything like that again. You wondered what exactly happened that made this deal a winner. When did the tide turn in your favor, and why?

Of course, you've tried again and again to replicate that deal. But so far, it's been hit or miss—and you've never done anything quite as good as that deal. It was your biggest deal, and it might remain your biggest deal, unless you answer the call to make deals like Warren Buffett.

We certainly are not going to tell you how to replicate that deal. To us, *replicate* is just another way to say "stagnate." And in deal making, stagnation is the kiss of death. Besides, you can't replicate it. The circumstances of that deal were unique. No two deals are exactly alike, so replicating one isn't possible.

No, what we want you to do is something else entirely. We're going on a journey to let you be able to make deals like the greatest dealmaker of all time.

This quest is to land a deal that you can't even imagine yet—it's that big. It might be $10,000, $1 million, or $100 million. It might be with a private company, or it might be with one of the Generals (like General Electric, General Mills, or General Motors).

No matter what size company you have, you can land your Warren Buffett kind of deal. What we outline in this book will guide you through a successful quest. If you follow the lessons and apply them to your situation, your deal-making prowess is bound to improve along the way.

This book isn't about incremental and slow growth. It's about explosive, major growth through key account selling. Equally important, it's about explosive, major growth time and time again. Making a deal like Warren Buffett is not a one-trick pony. It's a mindset, a set of principles, and some very effective strategies that you can use again and again.

=== WARREN WAY 1 ===

Opportunity Attracts Money

"Money will always flow toward opportunity, and there is an abundance of that in America," Warren Buffett told his stockholders in 2011.

Please understand we are not saying that this is going to be easy. Something that's worth achieving seldom comes easily. We will outline for you the importance of the challenges you will face; give you some concrete, tactical ways to meet them; and tell you stories about Warren Buffett and other dealmakers who have been extremely successful in landing big deals that have transformed their companies, their careers, and their causes.

We are confident that anyone who meets—or surpasses—these challenges will land his own version of a Warren Buffett–style deal. The reason we are confident is that we've seen it work with unimaginable success time after time.

Over the years, we have been very fortunate to work with many marvelous clients who have graciously allowed us to tell you about their experiences. So you'll find client stories interspersed throughout the book. We use these stories as examples, of course, but also as a tribute to the dedication and hard work our clients have exhibited time and time again. They provide us with a large portion of our inspiration on a daily basis. And for that, we are truly grateful.

Warren Makes Deals Differently

If you want to know about making big deals, Warren is still the guy to watch. Why? The man knows how to talk about money when he's making deals.

Warren does deals differently from the average businessperson. For those who want a road map on how to make bigger and better deals, the lessons contained in the following chapters will show you the Warren way.

Warren is famous for doing enormous deals with as little information as a few pages of business plans and the standard financials that a company would submit to a bank in order to qualify for a loan. However, what he has when he goes into any conversation is an encyclopedic knowledge of how businesses work financially. He knows

WARREN WAY 31

Learn from Others

Buffett credits many people that he has learned from along the way, such as his professor at Columbia Business School, Ben Graham, and his partner at Berkshire Hathaway, Charlie Munger. "You don't have to think of everything. It was Isaac Newton who said, 'I've seen a little more in the world because I stood on the shoulders of giants.' There is nothing wrong with standing on other people's shoulders."

"their money," "their wallet," and how investments and outcomes should work. Follow his lead, and you will close more business.

We are unabashed Warren watchers. We own stock in his company, read his chairman's letters in the Berkshire Hathaway annual reports, and devour news reports on the man. Our interest is not in studying his investment wisdom, but in decoding how the man makes a deal. Here are just seven deal-making traits to emulate that we have learned from watching Warren from afar:

1. *Know the other guy's money.* Warren always seems to know how the people he's dealing with make it, how they count it, and how they spend it. This is obviously much easier to do for publicly traded companies. For privately held companies, some of the numbers are fairly easy to estimate—at least the cost of goods sold and probably the cost of sales. These numbers are critical to discussing the possibilities of working together. Too often, the discussion stops at the budget. When you don't know, ask. Don't ask for trade secrets, but at least ask for the industry averages. This provides a basic framework for the discussion.

2. *Know the other guy's wallet.* How would this sale affect any of these critical numbers? The terms of the deal should be looked at from the other guy's side of the table first, then from yours.

3. *Start discussing the money early.* You know you are going to discuss the money in more detail later. Early in the conversation, you do not have enough information for precision. Instead, you need to have an understanding of the economics of the prospect's industry so that you have enough information to determine if a deal makes any sense at all. Use that economic information and industry knowledge to frame a shared understanding of the reality of the money for this opportunity.

4. *Use ranges to qualify and disqualify.* Understand early (and throughout the discussion) whether you and your prospect are in the same arena. By using ranges of prices, cost structures, yields, and performance, you can both be sure that you are dealing in a shared

reality rather than getting to the end and finding yourselves so far apart that permanent damage has been done to the relationship.

5. *Speak the language of investment and outcomes.* Every large sale is an investment in an outcome by both sides. When you move the conversation from price to investment and from cost to outcomes, you are focusing on the business impact rather than the budget impact. This is the language of large sales.

6. *Don't discount early.* If you listen carefully, you will regularly hear fearful "dealmakers" use language like, "Let's not let money get in the way of working together." There's a word for this that is not used in polite company. This is the language of discounting before the scope has been clearly defined. The salesperson believes that she is being clever by taking money off the table. What she has really done is to take margin off the table, her and her company's margin. If the deal qualifies as an investment and its impact has been determined up front, then this point does not need to be made again.

7. *Don't negotiate until it's time.* Work on the deal points one at a time. Work through the investment and outcome ideas clearly, then negotiate. True, all of these points require negotiation. However, too often the conversation turns to negotiation too early, before the real scope and deliverables have been defined. That means that the whole is reduced to the little parts before the shared picture of the whole has been established.

In the pages ahead, you will read many tales of deals that illustrate important lessons about how to make a deal like Warren Buffett. With each lesson, you will also get some specific thoughts on how to put the lesson into practice. No book about Warren would be complete without a generous amount of the wit and wisdom of the world's greatest dealmaker, which we include in our Warren Ways. And Warren has so much to teach us from a lifetime of deal making that we end each lesson with a Buffett Bonus.

Buffett Bonus | People Are as Important as Profits

If you talk to people who have made deals with Buffett, you will hear a recurring theme: to him, the people in the deal are as important as the financial metrics. That's because financial metrics reveal what has happened at a certain moment, but people are performers over time. Warren doesn't do hostile takeovers, turnarounds, or mergers. He makes deals for ongoing businesses that have proven managers in place to run them. In a Warren deal, the money counts, but the people count more.

LESSON 2

Go Big

WARREN BUFFETT is not afraid to go big. Back in 1986, he acquired the Scott Fetzer Company, a collection of 22 separate businesses. Scott Fetzer produced everything from Ginsu knives and the *World Book* encyclopedia to Kirby vacuum cleaners and Scot Laboratories' cleaning products. The deal was one of Warren's largest up to that point, and it has well exceeded his high expectations.

"We paid $315.2 million for Scott Fetzer, which at the time had $172.6 million of book value," Warren wrote in his 1994 letter to Berkshire shareholders. "The $142.6 million premium we handed over indicated our belief that the company's intrinsic value was close to double its book value."

In 1974, Ralph Schey, a Harvard Business School graduate, had become president of the company. Schey quietly grew the company into a cash flow dynamo. In the takeover craze of the go-go 1980s, however, Scott Fetzer's plump profit margins could not go unnoticed.

In 1984, takeover financier Ivan Boesky began accumulating shares of the company. A Schey-led group then announced a plan to take the company private in a leveraged buyout. Meanwhile, Kelso & Company, a New York investment firm, entered the hunt with a $61-a-share bid. Kelso's specialty was corporate buyouts through employee stock ownership plans (ESOPs), and the bid was raised to $62 a share by early 1985. Eventually the ESOP plan was scuttled.

At the time, Scott Fetzer was becoming widely known as being well managed and a good earner, two of Warren's favorite qualities. Not only was Warren on the prowl for companies with consistent earnings that he would not have to micromanage, but he also favored nontechnical industries that could be easily comprehended.

After the ESOP plan fell through, Warren wrote to Schey, saying that he admired the company's record. In typical Warren fashion, he did not hesitate to make a deal, even for a conglomerate of this size. Just a week after their first dinner together, the acquisition was signed.

Here is how Warren described the deal and his admiration for Schey in the 1994 letter to shareholders:

> *The difference between Scott Fetzer's intrinsic value and its carrying value on Berkshire's books is now huge. As I mentioned earlier—but am delighted to mention again—credit for this agreeable mismatch goes to Ralph Schey, a focused, smart and high-grade manager. The reasons for Ralph's success are not complicated. Ben Graham taught me 45 years ago that in investing it is not necessary to do extraordinary things to get extraordinary results. In later life, I have been surprised to find that this statement holds true in business management as well. What a manager must do is handle the basics well and not get diverted. That's precisely Ralph's formula. He establishes the right goals and never forgets what he set out to do. On the personal side, Ralph is a joy to work with. He's forthright about problems and is self-confident without being self-important.*

Schey stayed at the helm of Scott Fetzer until 2000. Scott Fetzer's performance validated Warren's reasons for buying the company. In the first 13 years after Warren made the deal to acquire Scott Fetzer, it netted more than $1 billion for Berkshire.

Solve Bigger Problems for Bigger People

If you want to make deals like Warren, you have to solve bigger problems for bigger people. It's as easy and as difficult as that. It follows, then, that your next Warren Buffett–style deal will require the following:

1. Identifying your prospect or prospects
2. Knowing your prospect's biggest problems
3. Pitching to the highest-ranked people in your prospect's company
4. Developing a solution for your prospect's biggest problems

But right at the start, let's have the money discussion.

WARREN WAY 17

Think Big or Go Home

At the beginning of an annual stockholders' meeting, Buffett tapped the microphone to see if it was on: "Testing... one million... two million... three million."

Set a Monetary Goal for Your Deal

Think of your Warren Buffett–style deal in terms of your last big deal. Would you like this one to be twice the size of that one? Or perhaps three times? Or ten? Or maybe one hundred times?

You want this number to be large enough to keep you focused and motivated during the hunt. If you set it too low, you may give up in frustration at some point, thinking that the deal's just not worth it. On the other hand, it has to be within the realm of reality. Just make certain that your current reality is not limited to the concept of selling more and more of your products or services.

"More and more" seldom works for big deals. It's natural to think in terms of landing your next big deal through selling more and more of your products or services. But the truth is that this is almost never an effective approach. Your next big deal needs to be a game-changing deal, not more of the same.

Currently, when you sell something to a buyer, you are solving an immediate problem. Your buyer needs something now. It's a finite number with a quick timetable. It can be as small as light bulbs or as large as prefabricated homes. It can be a workshop or a series of presentations on life insurance. The buyer needs it; you provide it. That's the extent of your deal, and you go on to the next one.

Of course, that's a huge generalization, but the point is that you have very little control over *when* this sale will take place or *what size* the order will be, two issues that are the essence of any deal. Both are controlled by the economy, the success of the buyer's business, customers' demands and lifestyles, or other factors. None of these elements are controlled or driven by you. That makes it extremely difficult for you to sell more and more to any one buyer. How can you make any buyer need more of your product or service at any given time? In truth, you can't. You may be able to find more buyers and sell to them, but they will be individual small deals, not the deal that you are going to make like Warren Buffett.

A second issue with selling more and more is the buyer you're currently dealing with. The chances are strong that he is a department manager with a limited budget. He can't unilaterally make the decision to purchase huge amounts from you. He can buy only what the company needs in his area. And what you're selling isn't a big enough problem to be solved in a big enough way to land your next big deal.

Take some time and think about your current deals. Consider the process you use and the people with whom you deal. At some point in your process, you can run into a roadblock that keeps you from making that big deal. It might be a person in the prospect company who dislikes you. It might be your dependence on railroads running on time for you to deliver your product. It might be your lack of knowledgeable IT people.

Whatever it is, that roadblock has the power to stop your deal. It becomes a factor that controls your deals.

It's obvious that you need to have a different approach if you want to land a Warren Buffett–style deal. That's what this book will give you. We are going to discuss a way for you to assert control over the deals you hunt and land. It takes you out of your current patterns and removes roadblocks before they appear.

Why Do I Have to Learn a New Way to Do Deals?

Making a Warren Buffett–size deal requires:

1. Working with a large number of people from the prospect company
2. Developing a solution and a message that have an impact on the entire company, not just one department
3. Enduring a long and often complex process
4. Selling to a prospect at the CEO or VP level with new attitudes and ideas
5. Gathering a team to work with you and attend meetings with prospects
6. Producing an opportunity that you make for yourself instead of waiting for the "right" opportunity to come along

If your current method of deal making includes the things in this list, then you're all set to land that big deal à la Warren Buffett. If not, read on.

We've asked salespeople around the country this question: "Are you going to sell a big deal this next year?" A common answer is, "I hope so. I hope the opportunity comes along soon."

Your big Warren Buffett kind of deal will not just "come along." You'll have to work to make it happen. You'll have to push your own envelope. Landing this kind of big deal requires a major shift in your selling approach. It also requires that you solve different problems from the simple one of "declared need = demand."

But relax. We're not going to suggest that you move from real estate to medical equipment or from advertising to technology. However, we will be suggesting that you adopt some new concepts and principles of selling.

Buffett Bonus | Trust Your Facts, Not the Group's Opinion

Big deals are not always good deals. You need to decide for yourself what deals you want to pursue. While doing a great deal of reading is vital, gathering the advice of others is not. In fact, Warren is wary of most opinions. In graduate school, he was amazed at how other students were willing to go with the flow of conventional wisdom. "I don't think there was one person in the class that thought about whether U.S. Steel was a good business. I mean, it was a big business, but they weren't thinking about what kind of train they were getting on." Warren does not believe in groupthink. "And the truth is, you are neither right nor wrong because people agree with you. You're right because your facts are right and reasoning right. In the end, that's what counts."

Consider Many, Like Some, Love Few

W ARREN LOOKS at many, many deals. Some of them he likes and pursues. When he finds one he loves, he moves fast.

For several years, one of Warren's managers, Nebraska Furniture Mart's Irv Blumkin, had been telling him about a furniture retailing giant in Utah, RC Willey. Blumkin had also told Bill Child, CEO of RC Willey, how pleased the Blumkin family had been with its relationship with Warren.

In early 1995, Child mentioned to Blumkin that for estate tax and diversification reasons, he and the other owners of RC Willey might be interested in selling. Warren quickly switched into deal-making mode.

"From that point forward, things could not have been simpler," wrote Warren in his 1996 letter to Berkshire shareholders. "Bill sent me some figures, and I wrote him a letter indicating my idea of value. We quickly agreed on a number, and found our personal chemistry to be perfect. By mid-year, the merger was completed."

Warren thought RC Willey's story was amazing. Child had taken over the business from his father-in-law in 1954, when sales were about $250,000. Aided by his brother, Sheldon, Child had built the company a hundredfold to a 1995 sales volume of $257 million, accounting for more than 50 percent of the furniture sales in Utah.

Like Nebraska Furniture Mart, RC Willey sold appliances, electronics, computers, and carpets in addition to furniture. Both companies had about the same sales volume, but Nebraska Furniture Mart generated all of its business from one megacomplex in Omaha, whereas RC Willey had opened five major stores and had a sixth on the way.

Warren loves businesses that are blessed with capable managers who love to compete and have done so successfully for decades. As he had done with the CEOs of his other operating units, Warren gave Child the green light to operate autonomously.

"We want them to feel that the businesses they run are *theirs*," wrote Warren. "This means no second-guessing by Charlie [Munger] and me. We avoid the attitude of the alumnus whose message to the football coach was: 'I'm 100 percent with you—win or tie.' Our basic goal as an owner is to behave with our managers as we like our owners to behave with us."

How to Know What the Right Deal Looks Like

When you try to think of your biggest prospect ever, an initial idea is to think of selling to huge companies, or, as we call them, "logo" companies. In rare cases, that works, but selling to these companies generally isn't a good strategy.

Sure, Warren Buffett made deals to take large positions in Coca-Cola, American Express, and Gillette. But those are not the deals that made him the greatest dealmaker in the world. Many of the companies he bought were hardly household names.

Going after big companies instead of big deals can be a recipe for disaster. You know the companies we mean, like Walmart, the U.S. Air Force, General Electric, or UPS. They're very well known and very large, and getting a big deal there will raise the eyebrows of all your colleagues and your competition.

Nevertheless, *never* go after the company. *Always* go after the deal.

If your next Warren-style deal ends up involving one of those companies, that's one thing. But don't try to force that situation to happen. If you do,

you'll end up frustrated and unhappy. All the eyebrow raising in the world won't compensate for the misery you may have to endure along the way. Here's why: logo companies move slowly.

Logo Companies Move Slowly

We were involved in trying to sell to a logo company once where we went to meeting after meeting, trying to see the buying authority. After we had spent days and weeks visiting with the company and meeting this person and that person, we discovered that its buying cycle was about 26 months. We were only four months into it, and we still hadn't met a single person who could make a buying decision.

And if it took 26 months to make a buying decision, how long do you think it would be before we cashed our first check from this deal?

We don't know about you, but we couldn't afford the luxury of pursuing the deal any further.

The buying cycles of logo companies are beyond patience, reason, or resources. These companies will bleed you dry, if you let them. We are reasonably sure that none of this is intentional. But logo companies are, by definition, huge. And with huge companies, there come many complications.

Logo companies have layer upon layer of people who seem to have to be involved in a buying decision. The first layer vets you and your solution on kind of a general level: your company's history, stability, reputation—that kind of thing. The second layer gets into more detailed conversations with you about your plans for solving the company's problems. But have you met an actual prospect yet? No. And you don't know how many more layers you have to go through.

So far, you've just been giving free consulting. You have no promise that the deal will ever go anywhere. And if you allow yourself to continue to spend inordinate amounts of time preparing reports, collecting data, and posing—and solving—hypothetical situations, you're acting like a fool. And fools don't win their next big Warren Buffett deal.

What Can Happen in Those 26 Months?

If it takes 26 months to close a deal, what can happen in the meantime? Given how quickly everything changes nowadays, the simple answer is, "Lots." Here are three good possibilities:

1. Perhaps the prospects will reorganize, and your deal will no longer exist.
2. Perhaps the CEO will leave, and the new one will take the company in a new direction.
3. Perhaps budgets will be cut drastically, and your deal will be the first to go.

You simply can't afford to spend so much time and money on such a dubious deal, all for the prestige of landing a logo company. Cuba Gooding didn't win the Academy Award in the film *Jerry McGuire* for saying, "Show me the prestige." He said, "Show me the money."

And here's a real kick:

The vast majority, and we mean vast, *of deals for seven figures or more end up with RFPs being sent out.*

After spending a large amount of time in the sales process, the company will often go ahead and issue an RFP. This happens much more often than you think. No matter how many meetings you've attended, this doesn't give you any advantage in the RFP process.

Many, if not most, Fortune 1,000 companies select the provider before they even send out the RFP. RFPs are not written with small to midsized companies in mind. If you respond to RFPs with minimum preparation, your success rate is likely to be 7 percent or lower.

After all that, you'll still probably end up with Procurement or Purchasing. Procurement and Purchasing have two things, and only two things, on their minds: (1) following all regulations and (2) money.

Let's do regulations first. There are lots of rules out there—and more of them every day—that logo companies are required to show that they followed when it comes to choosing major vendors. That's why they choose the RFP route so often. They have the paperwork that shows they did their due diligence before committing a huge sum of money to a vendor.

Do you ever think about regulations when you're pitching a sale? Of course not. And why should you? Buying process rules shouldn't be part of the sales process. Yet to logo companies, they are a huge consideration. Buying process rules dictate the way in which they make buying decisions.

As a result, these companies drag the process out for a long time and involve a lot of people to ensure they can show that they've done everything exactly right. You can't afford that.

Now, on to money. Procurement wants to get this deal for the smallest amount of money possible. You want this to be your next big Warren Buffett–type deal. In logo companies, Procurement will defeat you every time because of simple economics. You bring many, many attributes to this sale, but none of them is related to doing it for less.

There are situations in which you are glad to be dealing with Procurement or Purchasing. When operational efficiency is your clear business strategy and has provided you with a clear way to be the lowest-priced provider, then this approach can be your friend. For example, one of my clients, Echo Supply, had developed its value proposition around providing rubber molded parts from China. Echo was capable of providing U.S. engineering and quality control with Chinese labor costs and manufacturing plants. This put the company in a great position to win on a pure price quote basis. Procurement became a great point of entry for Echo. However, unless you have this type of strategy, I suggest you find another door.

Remember that buying process rules are not designed to help a company make a great decision. Instead, they are designed to help the company avoid a bad decision.

Stay Away from the "Back Door" Deal

You don't want to be part of a staff meeting where the CEO gathers everyone together and says, "We have to figure out how much loss we're willing to take just to get this deal. After all, it's Walmart, and if we can just get in the back door, it'll be easier to get other big guys. And it will get our name out there."

When we work with small and midsize companies, we often hear the siren song of the logo deal. This is not a discussion that I hear only occasionally. In one flavor or another, we hear this conversation in almost *every company* we meet. The promise of affiliated greatness for your brand because of someone else's strong brand is very hard to pass up. Believe me, I know.

Here's a quick summary of why this is a dangerous temptation.

1. *All hat, no cattle.* Your industry probably has a lot of companies that are doing business with these big players. Their websites and case studies are full of the logo-player company names. This means that you will be going to extreme lengths to get something that has little benefit because it is not unique.

2. *Black-hole prospects.* If you go after the big companies for their name, you are invariably going to be asked to do more, answer more, and spend more for a deal than you are used to. The never-ending requests and meetings can drain your resources, leaving you without those that are necessary to take advantage of other great opportunities with real scale and potential that aren't logo deals.

3. *What happens when the dog catches the car?* If you land a logo company and your company is not prepared to implement, you get to fail in a spectacularly public way.

Big Deals Make Your Team Crazy

Every deal is individual, of course, but there are certain things that all big deal teams have in common.

1. *There's always a fight.* Granted, it's a family fight, but it's a fight all the same. I have come to expect it and even to provoke it on occasion. If there isn't a fight, you have some potential bad mojo. Either

---

WARREN WAY 9

Have the Discipline of Ted Williams

From *The Essays of Warren Buffett*, which are drawn from his annual chairman's letters in the Berkshire Hathaway annual reports (available for free online): "We try to exert a Ted Williams kind of discipline. In his book *The Science of Hitting*, Ted explained that he carved the strike zone into 77 cells, each the size of a baseball. Swinging only at balls in his 'best' cell, he knew, would allow him to hit .400; reaching for balls in his 'worst' spot, the low outside corner of the strike zone, would reduce him to .230. In other words, waiting for the fat pitch would be a trip to the Hall of Fame; swinging indiscriminately would mean a ticket to the minors."

---

people aren't passionately engaged in the conversation and are just going through the motions, or people don't think you're going to be successful and are just going through the motions. Or, their mind is on something else, and again, they're just going through the motions. Bottom line: a fight is a good thing.

2. *Everyone is a mind reader.* People pull the tiniest scrap of data about people on the prospect's team and make an enormous projection about what those people want or will believe. Because of the desire to sell people at an emotional level, the more emotion there is connected to these scraps, the more these emotions become the focus of the discussion of what we should pitch. This can lead to some very dangerous conclusions. Start with the facts you know, then evaluate the opinions you have heard, and finally take a moment to consider the gossip. Just make sure you don't do it the other way around.

3. *Last-minute hijacking of the pitch.* At the eleventh hour, someone is going to stand up and say, "I think we've got this all wrong. We have to change this whole thing, or we might as well not bother pitching it." You can almost count on it. And these people win a lot more often than you would think. The fatigue of working through the process just starts to wear people out. The frustration of not being able to get it quite perfect will cause people to just give up on their current path and start over. Sometimes breakthroughs happen when frustration gives way to the release of creative energy. My caution is that if you cannot take the changes that are being offered and integrate them into the current pitch, don't switch your overall approach.

Try This Approach

So, if these things always happen, then what should you always do to manage these circumstances? Here are a few strong recommendations:

1. *Like Warren, be ruthless about the preparation.* Insist on giving all the data to all members of your team as early as possible. This includes a dossier on the target company, a profile of all participants in the buying process, and a copy of all communications regarding this deal.

2. *Pick your team early.* The team will shape the story, the key pitch points, the elements of Pitch Theater, the chemistry, the hunt process—all of it. Don't do the majority of the work and then bring the rest of your team in; you will only wind up with more fights and more hijacking this way.

3. *Set three meetings, minimum.* There is a deal strategy meeting. Then there is the pitch preparation meeting. Finally, there is the dress rehearsal or final review. These meetings need to be long enough to allow for vigorous discussion, a healthy fight, and brainstorming—so plan ahead.

4. *Assign roles.* People need to know up front what they will be responsible for. Who is handling communication with the client before and after the presentation or submitted solution? Who is responsible for creating the documents and pitch decks? Who will be the conductor during the pitch? If you assign roles early, people will do a better job of handling the job and of planning the time they need to do a good job.

Don't get us wrong; these recommendations won't completely fix things. We've seen our share of meeting hijackers and mind readers. These tips are about containing the energy and focusing it on what will help you to win.

Taking your team members through different kinds of maneuvers will guarantee that, when the real thing happens, they'll all know how to respond. And this is priceless.

Sometimes teams feel awkward when they're practicing, but don't worry. They'll begin to relax—and even enjoy the maneuvers—after a time. And once they find out how effective practice is, they'll insist on it every time.

Buffett Bonus | Deal for the Best, Leave the Rest

Warren says you need to love the deals you make and leave the others alone. "There are all kinds of businesses that Charlie [Munger] and I don't understand, but that doesn't cause us to stay up at night. It just means we go on to the next one," he said. But Buffett also understands the siren song of deal making. He once wrote: "Talking to *Time* magazine a few years back, Peter Drucker got to the heart of things: 'I will tell you a secret: Deal making beats working. Deal making is exciting and fun, and working is grubby. Running anything is primarily an enormous amount of grubby detail work…deal making is romantic sex. That's why you have deals that make no sense.'" That is probably why Buffett advises that if you smell a bad deal, do what you can to get out gracefully.

Bad Deals at Good Prices Are Still Bad Deals

IN 1962, Warren merged all his partnerships into one, then invested in and eventually took control of a textile manufacturing firm, Berkshire Hathaway, that would become his holding company. However, he regards the deal not as a great triumph but perhaps as his biggest deal-making blunder.

Buffett on Bargain Purchase Folly

"You might think this principle is obvious, but I had to learn it the hard way—in fact, I had to learn it several times over," Buffett wrote in his 1989 letter. "Shortly after purchasing Berkshire, I acquired a Baltimore department store, Hochschild Kohn, buying through a company called Diversified Retailing that later merged with Berkshire. I bought at a substantial discount from book value, the people were first-class, and the deal included some extras—unrecorded real estate values and a significant LIFO inventory cushion. How could I miss? So-o-o—three years later I was lucky to sell the business for about what I had paid. After ending our corporate marriage to Hochschild Kohn, I had memories like those of the husband in the country song, 'My Wife Ran Away with My

Best Friend and I Still Miss Him a Lot.' I could give you other personal examples of 'bargain-purchase' folly but I'm sure you get the picture: It's far better to buy a wonderful company at a fair price than a fair company at a wonderful price. Charlie [Munger] understood this early; I was a slow learner. But now, when buying companies or common stocks, we look for first-class businesses accompanied by first-class managements."

Hunting the Right Deals

Despite our dire warnings about logo-company deals in the previous lesson, we have to acknowledge that there can be some strategic value in doing business with a logo company. It does help other companies feel safer doing business with you when they see credible companies doing significant amounts of business with you. We've been involved in landing almost 200 of the Fortune 500 companies for seven-figure deals each over time, so we know that there is value in landing those names.

So let's talk about a strategy we've developed to provide you with the right balance of effort, result, and long-term leverage in your hunting efforts.

Let's assume that you are not selling to a logo company now, but you want to, or that you're selling to one and you want to move further up toward a bigger one. Then we suggest that you follow this logo deal strategy.

Start with Your Dream Deal List

First, think of those companies that you would like to do business with. If you're in the manufactured food business or a grocery-affiliated business, for example, that would be Walmart, Aldi, and

Kroger. But it's extraordinarily difficult to start with one of those companies. You have to work your way up to them.

Regardless of your business, there is a mega–Warren Buffett deal opportunity for you somewhere. That's the end you're shooting for. Pick your ultimate target. Make it a company that is big in size and big in name. There is nothing wrong with making it the richest family in town or one of the top 100 companies in the world. That target is yours to envision and name.

Second, you need to start with what your prospect needs. We'll use Walmart as an example (Tom recently made the trip to Bentonville, Arkansas, as part of a big hunt team). Walmart looks for the following in its vendors:

1. Proven ability to deal with sophisticated supply chain management systems that you don't control.
2. Proven ability to work on a national basis.
3. Proven ability to handle fluctuations in volume requirements by store, by city, and by region.

Other megastores may have different areas in which they want to see proven ability. But the point is that they all want to see it, and you'll have to provide it. Take each of these requirements and decide which of your current clients can provide the proof that Walmart is looking for. Make one list for systems, one for national footprint,

=== WARREN WAY 19 ===

Deal Making Is a No-Called-Strike Game

Buffett says, "You don't have to swing at everything—you can wait for your pitch." Buffett is fond of baseball and often uses the game to illustrate his philosophy. In deal making, you get to stand at the plate all day, and you never have to swing. Sometimes the best deals are the ones you don't make.

one for volume fluctuations, and so on. By the time you are presenting to Walmart, you will have a clear 360-degree capacity to meet its requirements.

Third, in what areas must you demonstrate success with increasingly more credible and sizable companies in order to make logo companies feel safe in hiring you? What do they want to see from the work you have done with the companies that preceded them? Primarily, they want safety and credibility. For most businesses, these come in the following categories:

1. *Geography.* What areas do you cover in distribution and service, and who are you serving with that coverage right now? If geography is important, it's critical that you demonstrate first regional capability, then national, and then international. If you are a regional player who tries to leap to a claim of serving companies in China, you are going to have a very hard time demonstrating credibility.

2. *Scale.* This is the language of pure capacity and volume. We like to say that volume has its own complexity. *Do not* assume that prospects will make the following logic leap: *If* you can do 10,000 units of product, *and* you have available capacity in your operation to do 100,000 units, *then* you can handle 100,000 units of volume. They won't. They know that you have to move through thresholds of volume to get to full capacity and that each threshold will have its own challenges. You have to get past several thresholds before you are going to get the full volume opportunity.

3. *Technology.* Prospects want to know that your systems will interface with theirs and that you have worked with systems like theirs before. Moving from smaller to larger clients over time will demonstrate your improving sophistication and your capability to interface with more complex systems.

4. *Certification of quality.* Certifications create a sense of outside validation for your operations that allows larger clients some breathing room when they are thinking about doing business with you. Without these certifications, their risk goes up dramatically.

5. *Financial stability.* Moving from $10 million in business to $35 million in business creates bubbles in your financial picture. Without demonstrated financial capacity and a history of profitable operations, your biggest opportunities are going to shy away. It is very damaging to these companies when a supplier gets into financial trouble, and they avoid such situations aggressively.

Start building a demonstrable capacity and significance in each of these areas to support your claims and show your effectiveness to your largest opportunities.

Fourth, connect the dots. Take the three Walmart requirements of success with systems, nationwide work, and volume fluctuations. Connect these requirements to the specific category that addresses it. Then connect that category to your current clients that can provide proof of your abilities in these areas.

Fifth, start from where you are. This works like the domino effect. To get to the final domino in the string, you have to tip the first one. To do that, you have to start from where you are. What clients do you have currently, and what do you demonstrate in your work with them that can get you to your first domino in the string?

The logo deal strategy is one of the most intentional approaches to true business development that we know. It puts you in the driver's seat for reaching your ultimate goals. The alternative that we see too often is that you call on everyone and hope that the big one will come in. And that's not a strategy.

Look for your strongest potential prospects among companies with the following characteristics:

1. Big enough to be your next big Warren deal financially
2. Innovative enough to listen to—and buy—your solution
3. Stable enough to follow through with full implementation

Remember, Warren Buffett didn't care that Scott Fetzer had more than 20 (dare we say boring) companies that were far from household names. He made the deal because the deal was the right deal. So always go for the deal, not the size of the company.

Buffett Bonus | Money Doesn't Care Where It Came From

Sometimes the best deals are the ones you don't make. Marquee names on the client list are nice, but money doesn't care where it came from. The best way to measure your business success is not by the logos, but by the zeros, as Buffett does. The *Harvard Business Review* reported on a 1994 letter to Berkshire Hathaway shareholders in which Buffett commented on the ego of big deals. "Some years back, a CEO friend of mine—in jest, it must be said—unintentionally described the pathology of many big deals. The friend, who ran a property-casualty insurer, was explaining to his directors why he wanted to acquire a certain life insurance company. After droning rather unpersuasively through the economics and strategic rationale for the acquisition, he abruptly abandoned the script. With an impish look, he simply said, 'Aw, fellas, all the other kids have one.'" Following what others do is not Warren's style. He has spent his life going against the grain. In deal making, he espouses, "to thy own self be true." Think for yourself, and don't get caught up in the herd mentality. "Would you rather be the world's greatest lover and have everyone think that you are the world's worst lover? Or would you rather be the world's worst lover and have everyone think that you are the world's best lover?" Also know that research isn't everything. Buffett writes, "If past history was all there was to the game, the richest people would be librarians."

LESSON 5

Deal Only with Dealmakers

DORIS CHRISTOPHER never dreamed that borrowing $3,000 on a life insurance policy would lead to her making a megadeal with Warren Buffett.

In 1980, when Christopher was 34 and living in Illinois, she began looking for a way to earn money while staying at home with her daughters, who were 5 and 8. She was an avid entertainer, and her friends often asked about her kitchen tools. Trained as a home economist at the University of Illinois, she knew how to find and use the best kitchen utensils.

Selling utensils sounded like a good idea, but how? She mentioned in-home parties instead of opening a store, and her marketing executive husband, Jay, embraced the idea. He suggested that she could redefine the direct-marketing concept.

Capitalizing on her knowledge of food preparation techniques and her natural talent for teaching, Christopher amassed an inventory of what she considered to be the essential home kitchen tools, promoted them under the name the Pampered Chef, and began showcasing them at in-home cooking demonstrations called cooking shows.

By 2002, the company, as Ellyn Spragins noted in *Fortune Small Business*, "sold $3.50 vegetable peelers yet has revenues of $740 million a year."[1]

While it has been said that Warren followed the money and it led him to Christopher's doorstep, actually she reached out to him in a letter (with a little help from Goldman Sachs).

She explained that the Pampered Chef, with headquarters in Addison, Illinois, served 12 million customers nationwide and had 71,000 independent sales representatives, called kitchen consultants, who sold its products through home-based party demonstrations, mainly in the United States. A party with 10 guests might sell $1,100 worth of kitchen tools. A consultant who agrees to open her kitchen for a party with friends may receive $250 to $300 in products for free. The consultant must pay $90 for a starter kit of tools, which the company says it values at $350; then she can collect a commission of 20 percent on her sales. If she recruits others into the sales network, she can collect 1 to 4 percent on their sales. Top performers are treated to weekend hotel stays.

Warren made the deal with Christopher to acquire the Pampered Chef, which had become the largest direct seller of kitchen tools in the United States. "Warren was wildly smart, knew the numbers, and spoke with total candor," recalled Christopher in a 2012 interview at the Berkshire Hathaway annual meeting. She said that when he made the financial offer, it was obvious that he valued great managers, and in the discussions, he stressed that "people were the key to success."

When the deal was announced, Warren said: "We are extremely excited by the Pampered Chef. Doris Christopher has created from scratch an absolutely wonderful business."

What was in the recipe for Warren to like? For starters, the Pampered Chef had no debt, high profit margins, an enthusiastic management team, and world markets to conquer. And the concept was simple and something that Warren could relate to.

The Pampered Chef gets women and men to sell kitchen products like peelers and whisks through in-home parties, a direct-sales system that's been used for decades by companies such as Tupperware and Mary Kay. The in-home parties push product, of course, but guests also are treated to recipes, utensil demonstrations, and homespun cooking tips.

According to *Fortune*, Christopher came across more as an understanding mom than a highly successful businesswoman. Yet from 1995 to 2001, Pampered Chef's revenues grew 232 percent, compared with 49 percent for the industry. The company had never had any debt, save for that $3,000 life insurance loan that Christopher and her husband used for the launch.

The Name of the Game Is to Find That Dealmaker

You can't land your next Warren Buffett big deal by selling to the same types of people in the same size companies at the same level of organizational authority. You've already gotten as much out of that approach as you can. Your prospect is higher up the food chain and has a different problem. You have to think the way that prospect thinks if you're going to make a Warren kind of deal.

For your next big deal, you'll need to sell to the executive-level person who has the perspective on the problem you can solve, such as the CEO or some other high-level executive officer. You need

---

WARREN WAY 30

Nobody's Perfect

Don't expect perfection from those you are making deals with or from yourself. Be willing to make mistakes now and then. Warren said, "I make plenty of mistakes and I'll make plenty more mistakes, too. That's part of the game. You've just got to make sure that the right things overcome the wrong ones."

---

someone with a larger budget, more flexibility, and more impact on the entire company.

It breaks down like this:

1. *Managers* think about their suppliers as providers of products or services. They make their decisions based on budget, ease of working with the vendor, amount of effort required to switch vendors, and whether the product or service will work in their current operation. A manager's goal is to make his day-to-day operations work with little change and some incremental improvement as measured by the boss's scorecard. Managers' problems revolve around price, service, and quality.

2. *Directors* think about changes in systems and processes that will make their departments have more capacity, increase their efficiency, and increase their speed. They think less about budget and vendor approval than managers do. They are measured on numbers both in and out of budget. Their problems are about yield, throughput, and ratios.

3. *Senior executives* think about moving the needles of market share, profit, and share price. These measures drive budget, which means that they are *outside* of budget. Executives' problems involve speed to market, first-mover position, and bottom-line impact.

True Story

An executive we know was in front of a famous congresswoman, selling her on the need for funding of a program that would help dramatically reduce carbon emissions from cars. He asked for the amount of money he needed, which was $3 million.

She said, "I think we can do the $3 *billion* you are asking for."

He laughed and said, "No, I'm sorry, I said $3 million, not $3 billion."

She stood up, said, "How the hell did I get into this meeting?" and walked out. She knew there was no way she could move the big measures she was responsible for moving with a $3 million investment. He was pitching at manager level, but he was talking to someone who was at senior executive level. Big people with big problems don't buy little solutions.

Case Study: Primary Sourcing

Finding out what the company dealmaker values can be a difficult task. An example comes from Primary Sourcing, a 15-year-old equipment engineering and manufacturing company for the oilfield services industry. It solves manufacturing problems within the tolerances of medical devices and rocket ships and has a reputation for making equipment that works in very inhospitable places.

An example would be the following: creating a perfectly accurate clock that can function two miles under the ocean's surface and then another mile into the earth's core, at 300°F, 3,500 psi pressure, with the kinds of vibration that would shake the fillings out of your teeth in fewer than a couple of seconds.

Obviously, during oil and gas boom periods, oilfield services companies can't get enough equipment to explore and drill everywhere they want to, so their balance sheets show tremendous liabilities in the form of outgoing expenses. And Primary Sourcing has a lot of work.

But during periods of lower prices, these same companies have too many assets on their balance sheets—too much equipment, components, and work in process (WIP). As a result, Primary Sourcing has little work to do.

For Primary Sourcing's prospects—CEOs at the oilfield services companies—the extreme fluctuations on their balance sheets made the companies look less stable than they really were. So Primary Sourcing decided to even the balance sheets, both for itself and for its clients. By finding a solution to the CEO-level concerns of its clients, Primary Sourcing found its next Warren Buffett kind of deal.

By purchasing the component inventory and work in process these service providers had in stock for its equipment and then performing that same manufacturing under contract, Primary Sourcing was able to solve both sides of the equation.

When the market is booming, Primary Sourcing can engineer and manufacture the equipment on an outsourced basis, meeting all the specifications necessary for that highly demanding customer base. When the market is down, Primary Sourcing moves the inventory off its customers' balance sheets so that its financial picture is stronger and its capital is more easily deployed.

Because the ownership of the components and WIP is contractually bound to the customer, Primary Sourcing's risk is almost zero, yet its partnership value to its customers is very high.

This evens out the market fluctuations for both companies. That is a win-win all the way around. That's the kind of solution you get when you focus primarily on dealing with the dealmakers.

Buffett Bonus | Make Deals with Passionate Dealmakers

Deal only with those who believe in their products and services. Buffett said: "I don't want to be on the other side of the table from the customer. I was never selling anything that I didn't believe in myself or use myself."

LESSON 6

The Language of Big Deals

"WE MADE a sizable acquisition in 1991—the H. H. Brown Company—and behind this business is an interesting history," wrote Warren in that year's letter to shareholders.

In 1927, a 29-year-old businessman named Ray Heffernan purchased H. H. Brown Company, then located in North Brookfield, Massachusetts, for $10,000 and began a 62-year career of running it. When Heffernan retired in early 1990, H. H. Brown had three plants in the United States and one in Canada, employed close to 2,000 people, and earned about $25 million annually before taxes. Brown (which, by the way, has no connection with the Brown Shoe Company of St. Louis, maker of Buster Brown shoes) was the leading North American manufacturer of work shoes and boots

Along the way, one of Heffernan's daughters married Frank Rooney, who was sternly advised by Heffernan before the wedding that he had better abandon any ideas he might have about working for his wife's father.

According to Warren, that was one of Heffernan's few mistakes: Rooney went on to become CEO of rival Melville Shoe Corporation. During his 23 years running Melville, from 1964 through 1986, the company's return on equity averaged more than 20 percent and its stock (adjusted for splits) rose from $16 to $960. A few years after

Rooney retired, Heffernan, who had fallen ill, asked him to run Brown.

When Heffernan died in 1990, his family decided to sell the company. Rooney gave the assignment of selling Brown to a major investment banker, which, in typical fashion, failed to think of Warren as a potential buyer. In one year, Warren bought four companies represented by investment bankers, and in three instances he had to initiate the deal.

But then Rooney played a round of golf in Florida with John Loomis, a longtime friend of Warren's and a Berkshire shareholder who is always on the alert for something that might fit Warren's taste in deals. Hearing about the impending sale of Brown, Loomis told Rooney that the company should be right up Berkshire's alley. Rooney, who had met Warren, promptly gave him a call.

"I thought right away that we would make a deal and before long it was done," Warren wrote. The key was speaking Rooney's language and getting him to stay on.

Warren understood shoes and knew that this was a tough business. The wide range of styles and sizes that shoemakers offer causes inventories to be heavy; substantial amounts of capital are also tied up in receivables. In this kind of environment, says Warren, only outstanding managers like Rooney and the group developed by Heffernan can prosper. Perhaps what impressed Warren the most was the company's compensation system:

A distinguishing characteristic of H. H. Brown is one of the most unusual compensation systems I've encountered—but one that warms my heart: A number of key managers are paid an annual salary of $7,800, to which is added a designated percentage of the profits of the company after these are reduced by a charge for capital employed. These managers therefore truly stand in the shoes of owners. In contrast, most managers talk the talk but don't walk the walk, choosing instead to employ compensation systems that are long

*on carrots but short on sticks (and that almost invariably
treat equity capital as if it were cost-free). The arrangement
at Brown, in any case, has served both the company and its
managers exceptionally well, which should be no surprise:
Managers eager to bet heavily on their abilities usually have
plenty of ability to bet on.*

Warren and Rooney's conversation centered around creating a
game that the incumbent CEO wanted to play.

"Much of my enthusiasm for this purchase came from Frank's
willingness to continue as CEO," wrote Warren. "Like most of our
managers, he has no financial need to work but does so because he
loves the game and likes to excel. Managers of this stripe cannot be
'hired' in the normal sense of the word. What we must do is provide a concert hall in which business artists of this class will wish to
perform."

How to Speak Big Deal

We don't often think of language as being an issue between us and our
prospects, but with your Warren Buffett–style deal, it definitely is.

Why? There are two reasons:

1. You're selling a solution to a bigger problem that your bigger
   prospect has.
2. You'll sell one or more steps up on your prospect's organization
   chart—at the executive level.

The prospects you used to focus on had budgets set in advance for
those goods and services that they needed. In those days, you would
go into their offices and say something to the effect of, "You're buying X number of widgets from my competitor. You should buy those
widgets from me now because mine are better, they're less expensive,
I handle my inventory more efficiently, and I provide services that my
competitor can't match."

Even more, you had the advantage of a "heads-up" against any existing competition out there.

You probably sold your product or service using the following:

1. Advantages your product or service brings to the prospects
2. Relieving prospects' pain
3. Your special features
4. The superiority of your methods
5. Prospects' issues with former vendors
6. Words like *quality, service, capacity, innovation, on-time delivery,* and *guarantees*

All of this is what the department manager was expecting to hear. Everyone was programmed to talk about service, quality, and price, so you emphasized those areas. It was appropriate language for *small deals.*

And these characteristics are important—*to the department manager,* whose responsibility is to serve as the gatekeeper for the department. Managers are expected to check and double-check all the characteristics you offer as evidence of the strength of your solution. If they don't, they lose their jobs.

But now you're going to sell to higher-level company dealmakers, the kind who occupy the C-level suites. Since they have delegated matters of service, quality, and price to the department manager, they have no interest in hearing about those subjects.

========================= WARREN WAY 14 =========================

Know the Language of Business Accounting

"When managers want to get across the facts of the business to you, it can be done within the rules of accounting. Unfortunately, when they want to play games, at least in some industries, it can also be done within the rules of accounting."

Money, Time, and Risk

The big dealmakers want to hear about *money, time,* and *risk.* These words are part of the language of big deals.

These are different deals with different prospects. Therefore, the language is different.

That doesn't mean that you have to repeat those exact three words in every other sentence. It means that you translate your solution descriptions into terms that clearly relay what is of most interest to your prospect. Here's how it works.

When you mention the quality of your products and services, what do you really mean? If you're talking about all your certifications of quality, while they're important, they aren't what the executives want to hear about.

It isn't that they don't care about quality. Of course they do. But for higher-level executives, their concern about quality takes a different form.

What does high quality mean to high-level executives? From their perspective, if they do a deal with you and you have high-quality products, what do they get?

Money
1. More repeat purchases from their customers
2. Reduced waste in production
3. Ability to price their products or services above those of their competition

Time
1. Trust that you will meet your deadlines
2. Fewer hours spent dealing with customer complaints
3. Quicker installation guaranteed to their customers

Risk
1. Less risk that they can't meet their deadlines
2. Less risk that their products or services won't work correctly
3. Greater customer confidence

You need to emphasize, and even quantify, these kinds of pluses in your solutions for C-suite executive problems. Saying that you have high-quality products or services doesn't do you any good; showing how their characteristics can be translated into money, time, and risk for the senior executives will give you a much better push toward landing your Warren Buffett deal.

Case Study: Digital Blue Global

Let us give you an example of a company that wanted to grow, so the salespeople went to a higher-level prospect with a different language and were successful with their next big Warren Buffett–style deal.

Our client, Digital Blue Global, produces events for groups like publishers, trade associations, and multilevel marketers. In the past, the company had pitched only to event planners. So, what are event planners most interested in?

1. Date
2. Time
3. Place
4. Cost of labor and materials
5. No problems

To event planners, a meeting or event has finite boundaries: it's at a specified time, on a certain date, in a selected place, costing a particular amount of money. A budget is specified. Then the event is over, and that's it.

Event planners aren't interested in the larger problems of the entire organization. They do exactly what their name says: they plan events.

However, simply producing events didn't satisfy Digital Blue Global. It had the capabilities to do much more than that for a client, in terms of money, time, and risk. Pre-event digital advertising and promotion was one capability. Another was tracking attendees after the event, assessing their interest in the company sponsoring it, and keeping that interest alive. The company could provide sustainable content in audio and video format for sale or promotional use on the web. Digital Blue Global could also provide a sustained relationship with attendees through campaign management of digital content so that over the following months, attendees would be reconnected with speakers and ideas from the event.

So they changed the following:

1. *What they sold.* They changed *from* producing a single event *to* establishing long-term relationships with event attendees.

2. *Whom they sold.* They changed their target *from* event planners *to* senior-level executives.

3. *What language they used.* They changed *from* focusing on the specifics of a single event *to* focusing on money, time, and risk.

Money

- Pre-event advertising and promotion increase the number of people attending the event.
- Postevent tracking establishes a long-term relationship with the attendees, with great potential for revenue generation down the road.
- Audio and video materials created during the event are available for sale to attendees before they leave.

Time

- Postevent tracking begins as soon as the event is over, while the excitement generated there is still fresh in the attendees' minds.
- Real-time material creation links this excitement to money at the point of impulse buying.

Risk

- Databases are confidential and shared with no one outside the customer company.
- Flawless execution means that the event moves from a meeting to an experience.

Digital Blue Global is still quite capable of handling a single event. But it no longer concentrates on doing only that.

Instead, Digital Blue Global now sells the complete package of what's valuable to its prospects—the pre-event promotion, production of the event, and postevent tracking. The combination of the three factors is what is of most value to Digital Blue Global's prospects. And prospects will pay much more to get all three.

Always think about the strengths of your deal first. *Don't* think about where the money to buy your solution will come from until you have the strengths defined.

Way too often, salespeople get discouraged and give up as soon as they hear the words "That's not in the budget for this year." They know the intricacies of developing a budget and getting approval for it. Nothing short of a major event can change the budget.

But budgets aren't made by salespeople looking for their next big deal. They may be developed by number crunchers who use this year's figures as a guide for next year's opportunities.

Your next Warren Buffett–style deal is not usually an item that is strictly defined by a line item in the budget.

Suppose you sell paper clips. Your line item may say "office supplies."

Now suppose you've figured out an office supply chain management system that will decrease overall expenses for office supplies and put greater controls into place to decrease waste. There's no line item for that. The budget just says "office supplies."

But if the prospect's biggest problems are cost and waste, and ways to cut both are major initiatives, then you've got a perfect solution. And when you present that solution, a way to pay for it, probably outside the budget, will be found.

Why? Because the deal maker values your deal, and dealmakers pay for what they value.

Buffett Bonus | Simplicity Has Elegance

Seek simplicity in deals. Don't overcomplicate agreements. "The business schools reward difficult complex behavior more than simple behavior, but simple behavior is most effective." Deal making shouldn't be difficult. "There seems to be some perverse human characteristic that likes to make easy things difficult." Buffett is adamant that you don't force deals. "You do things when the opportunities come along. I've had periods in my life when I've had a bundle of opportunities come along, and I've had long dry spells. If I get an idea next week I will do something. If not, I won't do a damn thing." In addition, every deal must be penciled out in advance. "You ought to be able to explain why you're taking the job you're taking, why you're making the investment you're making, or whatever it may be. And if you can't stand applying pencil to paper, you'd better think it through some more. And if you can't write an intelligent answer to those questions, don't do it."

On choosing deals that make sense: "I want to be in businesses so good that even a dummy can make money," Buffett told *Fortune* magazine in 1988. Warren advises not letting your deal-making reach exceed your grasp. "I don't try to jump over seven-foot bars: I look around for one-foot bars that I can step over," says Buffett.

Clear the Deal Path

I N 2003, thanks to a tip from some MBA students, Warren acquired the manufactured housing company Clayton Homes for $1.7 billion (or $12.50 per share). The numbers were great. Clayton operated 32 manufacturing plants in 12 states, and its homes were marketed in 48 states through a network of 1,540 retailers, 391 of which were company-owned sales centers.

But the deal was not as smooth as aluminum siding, and Warren had to work hard to clear the deal path. According to *Fast Company*, in 2004, the deal quickly led to shareholder litigation that alleged "self-dealing, abusive control and lack of candor." Despite the fact that the manufactured home industry was in one of the worst slumps in decades and Warren's acquisition price was 12.3 percent higher than the Clayton Homes share price at the time, there were still issues.[2]

Perhaps Warren's reputation for value investing was the reason behind the shareholders' hand-wringing. One opponent said that the fact that Buffett had made an offer was proof enough that it was a low-ball bid.

The Clayton Homes deal eventually received shareholder approval, but by a slim margin of 52.3 percent.

In making the deal, Jim Clayton received most of the public cheers (and jeers) for growing and then selling the company. What Warren understood was that while Jim Clayton had built the company in a rags-to-riches manner, it would be the next generation, his son Kevin Clayton, who would craft the company's future success. Warren made the deal because he liked the new master builder at Clayton.

Warren admits that his deals have often come about in strange ways. None, however, had a more unusual genesis than this deal to purchase a family business.

The unlikely deal architects were a group of business students from the University of Tennessee and their teacher, Dr. Al Auxier. For the previous five years, Professor Auxier had brought his MBA students to Omaha, where the group toured Buffett holdings like Nebraska Furniture Mart and Borsheims and then had a discussion session with Warren himself.

Usually about 40 students participated. After two hours of give-and-take, the group traditionally presented Warren with a thank-you gift. In past years, it had been items such as autographed footballs and other sports memorabilia from the university.

In his 2003 letter to shareholders, Warren explained a different type of present he had received.

This past February, the group opted for a book—which, luckily for me, was the recently-published autobiography of Jim Clayton, founder of Clayton Homes. I already knew the company to be the class act of the manufactured housing industry, knowledge I acquired after earlier making the mistake of buying some distressed junk debt of Oakwood Homes, one of the industry's largest companies. At the time of that purchase, I did not understand how atrocious consumer-financing practices had become throughout most of the manufactured housing industry. But I learned: Oakwood rather promptly went bankrupt. Manufactured housing, it should be emphasized, can deliver very good value to home purchasers. Indeed, for decades, the industry has accounted for more than 15% of the homes built in the U.S.

Upon receiving Jim Clayton's book, *First a Dream*, Warren told the students how much he admired the company's record and asked them to take that message back to Knoxville, home of both the University of Tennessee and Clayton Homes. The professor then suggested that Warren call Kevin Clayton, Jim's son and the CEO, to express his views directly.

"As I talked with Kevin, it became clear that he was both able and a straight-shooter," Warren later recalled. "Soon thereafter, I made an offer for the business based solely on Jim's book, my evaluation of Kevin, the public financials of Clayton, and what I had learned from the Oakwood experience. Clayton's board was receptive, since it understood that the large-scale financing Clayton would need in the future might be hard to get."

While that was how the deal was publicly portrayed, the behind-the-scenes action was a little different. According to the *Journal of Private Equity*, the students recommended the deal to Warren at the suggestion of the firm's founder and CEO, Jim Clayton, with the complicity of the professor. "Apparently, Mr. Clayton was 'rich in stock but relatively poor in cold hard cash,' which is a very good reason to seek a friendly acquisition."[3]

Two weeks later, the deal was done. "I made the deal over the phone without ever seeing it," Warren told the media.

Here's how Warren expressed his gratitude to the students for their thank-you gift, as detailed in the 2007 shareholders' letter.

And the students? In October, we had a surprise "graduation" ceremony in Knoxville for the 40 who sparked my interest in Clayton. I donned a mortarboard and presented each student with both a PhD (for phenomenal, hard-working dealmaker) from Berkshire and a B share. Al got an A share. If you meet some of the new Tennessee shareholders at our

annual meeting, give them your thanks. And ask them if
they've read any good books lately.

Today Clayton Homes, with more than 12,000 team members,
is the nation's largest retailer of manufactured homes. The modular
and manufactured homes are built in 35 U.S. building facilities and
distributed through a network of more than 1,500 home centers.
Clayton Homes also offers home financing, loan servicing, and insurance through several subsidiary companies.

How Rocky Will Your Deal Path Be?

The path to completing a deal is seldom smooth. If your next Warren
Buffett deal is big enough, it may require a major reorganization or
tackling some other issue. And your prospect will react with fear.
He may be enthusiastic about the idea, but fear can cancel that out.
You have to be prepared to deal with that fear.

Be sure you give the deal prospects tools that they can use to
defend their decision later. A major part of prospects' fear of commitment
is the conversation that's going on in their heads during the entire process.

=== WARREN WAY 29 ===

Plan for Rough Paths Ahead

Buffett says: "The roads of business are riddled with potholes; a plan that requires dodging them all is a plan for disaster."

You know exactly what we mean.
Nothing is articulated, but the prospects are having this conversation
in their heads while you're talking.
In their minds, three months in the
future, they're being challenged, by
someone whom you probably have
never met, about their buying deci-
sion. "Why in heck did you buy XYZ? Why did we change over
from the former systems to the new system? Do you have any idea
how much trouble that's causing in my department? Do you have any
idea how much additional expense there is?"

Too often, when offering a solution, presenters begin with a thorough attempt to make the prospect *understand* the product or service they are trying to sell. So they educate. They may spend a lot of time on small details in an endeavor to make the prospect understand exactly how everything works together.

The problem is, prospects don't buy just because they understand the product or service. You've heard it over and over: "Yes, I understand what you're saying, but our company is different."

So the potential vendor moves on to trying to make the prospects *believe* in the product or service. This time the approach has more passion: "I just want you to believe in what I'm telling you." So they persuade.

The problem is, prospects don't make deals just because they believe in the product or service. "Yes, I see what you're saying, and I believe it, but So-and-So just won't buy it."

What prospects do make deals on is *what they can sell and defend later.*

Not only must prospects understand and believe in the product or service, but they also have to be able to explain to some unknown and unseen person or group of people why they made that particular decision. You have to train and equip the prospect so that she can make an appropriate and useful defense later.

Dan Kemper from Schur Packaging Systems gives insight into this kind of real-life situation:

> *We had a prospect who was thinking of going with us over another vendor they had used in the past. So you can imagine the conversation that went on in their board room. "OK. Let me get this straight. You just bought from Vendor X over here, and now you want to go with not just a different vendor but also a vendor you've never worked with, for this new project? Please explain to me why you want to do that and why you are willing to go out on a limb for this. And all for more money. Where is your justification?"*
>
> *Oh, to be a fly on the wall in that type of situation.*

*They did go with us, but there was a lot of fear that had to
be eliminated first.*

Tool School Is in Session

Training and equipping prospects are done through providing tools
that the prospects can use to defend their choice of you as vendor.
Remember the adage about a picture being worth a thousand words?
Here are two examples.

1. *Schedule and safety indicators.* If you have consistently performed
on or ahead of schedule in similar projects, you should develop a tool
that will let you show this. A chart with a list of similar projects,
scheduled delivery dates, and actual delivery dates will work. If you
are a construction company and you can also include a large number
of days without injury or other delay, that would be useful, too.

2. *Process map.* Another tool is a visual illustrating your unique
process and steps that show how you accomplish your results quickly
and efficiently. The transparency this tool creates will demonstrate
another of your unique advantages.

Tip: Name That Tool

When you develop tools that prospects can use to defend their decisions
later, think about naming them. It takes very little time, and the name
doesn't have to be dreadfully alliterative or cute. When you present a
tool without a name, it comes across as an unsubstantial part of your
organization's procedures. A name gives the tool weight and suggests a
history of use. Even something as simple as the Apex Method for Smooth
Transitions can make the tool seem important. Never mind that it was
developed yesterday just for this project. It sounds as if it has been part
of your company's way of doing business for years. By doing this, you
will alleviate fear.

When you create tools, you give the prospect the chance to step right up and say, "Yes, I can tell you why I picked this vendor. Let me show you. Have you ever seen anything so organized and good for us?" This is exactly the discussion you want to facilitate.

Never limit your sales presentation to just educating and persuading your potential prospects. Doing so doesn't give them the ammunition they need if they are to buy. But their knowledge of and belief in what you are proposing can fool you into thinking that the sale is a done deal when it really isn't.

Go the extra step. Give them tools that they can use to prove the high value you are bringing to their company.

Making the shift from selling a product or service to selling a solution to a major problem is complicated and difficult. Nevertheless, it's a shift you have to make if you want to make deals like Warren Buffett.

Buffett Bonus | Smart Rather Than Clever

Most deals that Buffett makes are done with a minimal amount of complication. Typically, the whole deal can be written on one or two pages. He believes in dealing with trustworthy people rather than having 50-page ironclad contracts. Buffett believes it takes a lifetime to build a reputation, and you can destroy it in an instant. Your reputation for integrity is perhaps your greatest deal-making asset.

Getting to Dealmakers

Barnett Helzberg got the dealmaker of his dreams in a most unusual manner.

"My dream buyer for the family business all along was Warren Buffett," said Helzberg, the owner-manager of Helzberg Diamonds shops. "I knew we could trust him to keep the headquarters in Kansas City, resist changing the company's character, and retain the jobs of all of Helzberg's associates. It might have been simpler to sell to the highest bidder, but that notion seemed as sensible as choosing a brain surgeon based on the lowest price rather than on talent and reputation."

Now, Warren loves jewelry—not to wear, but to own as a business. Without a doubt, this was in the back of Helzberg's mind when he bumped into Warren Buffett in New York City.[4]

"As I walked past the Plaza Hotel near 58th Street and Fifth Avenue on a glorious May morning in 1994, I heard someone call out, 'Warren Buffett!' Turning in the direction of the voice, I saw a woman in a bright red dress stop Buffett on the sidewalk and start a friendly conversation with him. Buffett, dressed comfortably in an off-the-rack suit, listened patiently to the woman, who, it turned out, was a shareholder of Berkshire Hathaway, Buffett's hugely successful company."

Helzberg owned four shares of Berkshire stock at the time, with each share valued at "only" $20,000 (in 2012, shares were trading at more than $120,000). He recognized Warren from seeing him at the Berkshire Hathaway annual meeting. A fateful 30-second conversation ensued.

As busy New Yorkers rushed past them, Helzberg told the greatest dealmaker in the world why he should make a deal for Helzberg's family's 79-year-old jewelry business, headquartered in North Kansas City, Missouri.

"I believe our company matches your criteria for investment," Helzberg said. To which Warren replied simply, "Send me the information. It will be confidential."

Here is how Warren recalled the meeting, as described in an annual letter to shareholders:

> In our few minutes of conversation, Barnett said he had a business we might be interested in. When people say that, it usually turns out they have a lemonade stand—with potential, of course, to quickly grow into the next Microsoft. So I simply asked Barnett to send me particulars. That, I thought to myself, that will be the end of that. Not long after, Barnett sent me the financial statements of Helzberg's Diamond Shops. The company had been started by his grandfather in 1915 from a single store in Kansas City and had developed, by the time we met, into a group with 134 stores in 23 states. Sales had grown from $10 million in 1974 to $53 million in 1984 and $282 million in 1994. We weren't talking lemonade stands.

Warren quickly came to understand the other's guy's wallet. Helzberg, who was then 60, loved the business, but also wanted to feel free of it. In 1988, as a step in that direction, he had brought in Jeff Comment, formerly president of Wanamaker's, to help him

Warren, of course, quickly grasped Helzberg's moneymaking formula too. "The average Helzberg's store has annual sales of about

$2 million, far more than competitors operating similarly-sized stores achieve," Warren later recalled. "This superior per-store productivity is the key to Helzberg's excellent profits."

Warren perceived that the person on the other side of this deal felt that he owned a valuable asset that was subject to the vagaries of a single, very competitive industry, and believed that the prudent action was to diversify his family's holdings. Here is how Helzberg would later describe it.

"Personally, I felt uncomfortable expanding the company beyond my ability to know every store manager on a first-name basis," wrote Helzberg in his memoir, *What I Learned Before I Sold My Company to Warren Buffett.* "We had grown well beyond that point, and we were still growing. We had no interest in going public. We didn't want to be pressured to pay more attention to quarterly earnings and stock price than to the long-term operational health of the company and the well-being of our associates. We certainly didn't want some financial butcher carving up this jewel and selling it piecemeal. I also didn't want my associates spitting on my grave."

In the annual letter, Warren summed up the deal and the importance he places on having the right management in place.

> *Berkshire was made to order for him. It took us awhile to get together on price, but there was never any question in my mind that, first, Helzberg's was the kind of business that we wanted to own and, second, Jeff was our kind of manager. In fact, we would not have bought the business if Jeff had not been there to run it. Buying a retailer without good management is like buying the Eiffel Tower without an elevator.*

Typically Warren pays cash for a company. But Berkshire completed the Helzberg purchase in 1995 by means of a tax-free exchange of stock, the only kind of transaction, he said, that interested Helzberg. Warren also noted that although Helzberg was certainly under no obligation to do so, he shared a meaningful part of his proceeds from the sale with a large number of his associates. "When someone behaves that generously, you know you are going to be treated right as a buyer."

How well did Warren understand the other guy's wallet in this instance? According to Helzberg, extremely well.

How to Find the Big Wheel for the Big Deal

Warren has no problem getting to dealmakers. However, until you make that first $1 billion, you won't be so lucky.

What you need is a champion on the inside. Recruiting a champion is not that difficult, although it may seem that way at times. We want to introduce a method that has been used with great success by many of our clients.

═ WARREN WAY 47 ═

All It Takes Is a Few Right Deals

Buffett says: "You only have to do a very few things right in your life so long as you don't do too many things wrong."

Before you try to make any connection at all, you have to be thoroughly versed in exactly what you want to say. It's alarming how many people write an e-mail or push buttons on the phone before they know exactly what they should say. The result is that they don't get what they want.

So we'll start with your message, what we call *the Triples*.

Triple 1: Prospect's Three Problems to Be Solved

By now, we assume that you have a firm grasp on the problems you can solve for your clients. If you haven't done so already, take the time now to write those problems down in terms of money, time, and risk.

That's the language that champions want to hear.

Here is an example that illustrates perfectly how to approach the problems and how to begin communication.

Pretend you are a specialist in HVAC and energy cost reduction serving big-box retailers whose locations are larger than 150,000 square feet and who operate nationally. Your next big Warren Buffett prospect has identified the following three initiatives, among others, as the ones to be given maximum attention within the next year.

1. Reduce overall energy spending by more than 10 percent within the next year.
2. Get regulatory and tax-incentive approval on "green" initiatives.
3. Finish a higher percentage of projects ahead of schedule.

Let's look in more detail at what we've got here.

You have identified exactly what you do and to whom you sell. You have also identified the major current initiatives of your prospect company. You are aligned with the next big deal problems you solve and the prospect's biggest issues.

Triple 2: Your Three-Part Solution

Now you need to think about exactly how you solve these problems. No doubt you have found your solution already. Write it down in terms of the three problems you just identified. You have worked within your company to find your value, and you have attached a dollar amount to it in several ways.

Generic language such as *improved*, *better*, and *big difference* is not very compelling. So, you should use actual numbers, specific pressure points, and the type of goal wording that you saw in the prospects' initiatives. For example,

1. $250,000 first-quarter hard-dollar energy cost reductions
2. $500,000 tax credit for green initiatives
3. 97 percent on-schedule completion of installations

With these specifics, you have pinpointed specific outcomes that you can tell your prospect to expect. At this point, you've completed the second of the Triples.

Triple 3: Your Three References

The third step of the Triples is to identify at least three references you can use—people who have seen similar kinds of outcomes when they used your products or services.

This can be a sensitive area. Sometimes you have to be careful because of confidentiality agreements or internal agreements with your clients. Sometimes you can't talk about your customers because that might put them on their competitor's radar. Barring those limitations, we will say this: *the most effective way to get the attention of prospects is to drop the names of others just like them.*

We know you haven't done this kind of deal before. But certainly you have sold your products or services before, and you have customers that will give you glowing recommendations based on what they do know. Ask one reference to talk about what she knows about one area, such as your ability to save money for your prospects (money). Ask another one to talk about a different area, such as how quickly you delivered (time). And a third could talk about above-average safety and production records that show your ability to deliver ahead of schedule (risk).

Even though you haven't done this specific deal before, you can have references address different facets of the deals you've done with them, remembering always to couch them in terms of money, time, and risk.

Now you have all the parts for the Triples. These are:

1. Three problems of the prospect
2. Three solutions or outcomes from you
3. Three references to testify to your abilities

When it comes time for you to make your initial contact with your identified champion, the Triples provide you with an excellent way to get in. Here's why: you're talking about the very issues that your prospects have identified for their company. You're appealing to money, time, and risk when you cite your potential outcomes. And you're telling them that some other companies much like theirs have experienced positive outcomes from their work with you.

This is the type of message to which they'll respond and about which they'll want to hear more.

It's Not a Pain Discovery Mission

You've probably been taught throughout your sales career that it's your job to discover the prospect's pain. You're supposed to open up a dialogue with prospects, establish rapport, and then do discovery of what their pain is, right? Not for your next big Warren Buffett deal. The fact is, prospects for your next big deal expect you to have a relevant and valuable understanding of their problems so that you can discuss their general context immediately. That's why you take the strong position of identifying what the three problems and outcomes are.

The traditional approach of asking for time to "learn about you and see if there is a way that we can work together" will be brushed aside. You sound like a sales hack, not a potentially relevant and valuable solution to a problem that a truly credible source in the industry would already understand.

Initial Contact with Your Champion

Now we move on to the actual contact with your identified champion. This process has 10 steps. After the first three phone calls, you will have the choice of either continuing the pursuit of this company or stopping the pursuit; either way, the choice is yours to make.

The best way to make contact is by phone. It is possible that social media connections will allow you access; however, for now, your better point of access is still probably phone. Chances are that you'll get voice mail, so we've written out a script you can follow. Adapt this script to your own specifics and also to the possibility that you will get through to your potential champion immediately.

Step 1: Make the First Call

When you leave a voice mail, you will introduce the three problems you can solve. Do not leave a phone number or an e-mail address. You are going to establish trust by doing what you say you are going to do.

In the first call, you introduce the three problems you can solve. Say this:

Hello. This is _____, and I'm calling from XYZ Company, a specialist in HVAC and energy cost reduction serving big-box retailers whose locations are larger than 150,000 square feet and who operate nationally.

We help companies like yours that are working on the following three key areas: (1) reducing overall energy spending by more than 10 percent, (2) securing regulatory and tax-incentive approval for "green" HVAC initiatives, and (3) completing build-to-suit and retrofit new sites' HVAC design and installations ahead of schedule. I'll call again tomorrow at 9 A.M. I hope to talk with you then.

Step 2: Make the Second Call

When you leave a voice mail, introduce the outcomes you can deliver. Be certain that you make this second call at the exact time you said you would. Do not leave a phone number or an e-mail address. Say this:

Hi. This is _____, and I'm calling from XYZ Company, a specialist in HVAC and energy cost reduction serving big-box retailers whose locations are larger than 150,000 square feet and who operate nationally.

Working with companies like yours, we have produced key outcomes such as the following: (1) $250,000 first-quarter hard-dollar energy cost reductions, (2) a half-million-dollar tax credit on just three new facilities for "green" initiatives, and (3) 97 percent on-schedule completion of more than 300 HVAC installations in facilities over 150,000 square feet.

I'll call tomorrow at 9 A.M., and I hope to talk with you at that time.

Step 3: Make the Third Call

When you leave a voice mail, call at the exact time you said you would. This time, talk about your references. Do not leave an e-mail address.

Say this:

Hello. I'm _____, and I'm calling from XYZ Company, a specialist in HVAC and energy cost reduction serving big-box retailers whose locations are larger than 150,000 square feet and who operate nationally.

Companies like yours, including _____, _____, and _____, have used us to achieve these results. Please give me a call back at (phone number) so that we can talk about your needs. Thank you.

What to Do Next

At this point, prospects who are interested will usually call. Our clients report about a 40 percent callback rate after three calls. If you haven't gotten a callback, you have three choices at this point.

Choice 1: Think about getting a new champion. It's pretty clear that this particular person isn't as interested in your proposed solution as you need a champion to be.

Choice 2: Three taps and out; two months and back. You've made your three taps at this point, and your wisest course may well be to wait two months and then go back with the same system. Given how quickly changes can be made, you might be talking with a different person entirely. Or the company's circumstances might have drastically altered.

Choice 3: Follow steps 4 to 10. If you're not quite ready to put this away and wait for two months, you can follow steps 4 to 10.

Step 4: Call Two Days After Your Third Call

Leave a message similar to the one you left on the third call, and again leave your voice mail number. Do not leave an e-mail address.

Step 5: Call Two Days After the Fourth Call

Say this:

> *Identify yourself and say, "I'll be sending you today an e-mail with some facts and figures showing the ways we have helped other companies achieve their desired outcomes in the marketplace. I'm sure you'll see the long-term benefits of working with us."*

Step 6: Call the Same Day as the Fifth Call

Tell the prospect the facts, the figures, and, most important, the testimonials you have that demonstrate that you know how to help.

Step 7: Call Two Days After Fifth Call

Leave your company name and phone number, but mention, "Timing is always important, and for that reason, I'll put you in my tickler file to contact again in six months."

Step 8: Send the Prospect a Packet by Mail

Mail the prospect a packet about your firm, including your card and saying, "If you need anything, please feel free to call." Do not call. Do not e-mail.

Step 9: Five Months Later

If you are in the area, drop by and see the company five months later, referring to all of your voice mails and other communications. Say, "As you can probably tell from all my calls and notes, I'm really interested in meeting you." Don't call or e-mail.

Step 10: File This Prospect Away

After six months, file this prospect away for review in 90 days. Do not call, e-mail, or mail.

We have found this process remarkably effective, as we have used it with our clients and also heard their stories of success with it.

Buffett Bonus | Solid People Make for Solid Deals

Every deal that Buffett makes is sealed with a handshake. Then the lawyers come in and memorialize the details. If you are closing a deal with a bad person, there is no contract in the world that will protect you. Regarding types of deals, Buffett believes that great deals come from ideas that are tried and true. The ideas come from other people and businesses that have successfully put them to work. That's why he likes areas like insurance, building materials, and jewelry. He doesn't like new and risky areas such as technology and financial services.

Buffett was asked by CNBC about his interest in making a deal with candy giants Wrigley and Mars. "Well, I understand a Wrigley or a Mars a whole lot better than I understand the balance sheet of some of the big banks. I know what I'm getting in this, and some of the larger financial institutions, I really don't know what's there." He likes to make deals with people who have proven track records.

"You don't have to think of everything. It was Isaac Newton who said, 'I've seen a little more in the world because I stood on the shoulders of giants.' There is nothing wrong with standing on other people's shoulders."

When You Are Going to Eat an Elephant, Don't Nibble

W HEN WARREN made the jumbo deal to buy North America's second-biggest railroad in 2009, he called it an "all-in wager" on the U.S. economy. When that elephant-sized bet paid off big, one transportation industry analyst said, "It's just good luck." Those who study Warren would not chalk it up to mere good gambling fortune.[5]

Today's Burlington Northern Santa Fe (BNSF) is the product of nearly 400 different railroad lines that merged or were acquired over the course of 160 years. When Warren goes big, he goes big. BNSF operates in 28 states and 2 Canadian provinces. It is one of the top transporters of consumer goods, grain, industrial goods, and low-sulfur coal that help feed, clothe, supply, and power American homes and businesses every day. BNSF has developed one of the most technologically advanced and efficient railroads in the industry.

Here is how Warren did the math, as discussed in his 2011 letter to shareholders:

Measured by ton-miles, rail moves 42% of America's inter-city freight, and BNSF moves more than any other railroad—about 37% of the industry total. A little math will tell you that about 15% of all inter-city ton-miles of freight in the U.S. is transported by BNSF. It is no exaggeration to characterize railroads as the circulatory system of our economy. Your railroad is the largest artery. All of this places a huge responsibility on us. We must, without fail, maintain and improve our 23,000 miles of track along with 13,000 bridges, 80 tunnels, 6,900 locomotives and 78,600 freight cars. This job requires us to have ample financial resources under all economic scenarios and to have the human talent that can instantly and effectively deal with the vicissitudes of nature, such as the widespread flooding BNSF labored under last summer. To fulfill its societal obligation, BNSF regularly invests far more than its depreciation charge, with the excess amounting to $1.8 billion in 2011. The three other major U.S. railroads are making similar outlays.

In 2012, BNSF became the busiest railroad in the United States in terms of freight volume. BNSF's track network made it among the best located to meet the new needs of the energy industry, such as the demand for fracturing sand, pipe, and crude in the northern United States. The revenue leader, Union Pacific, was not as well situated to meet this demand because it lacks tracks into the area.

"It's kind of like if somebody discovers gold in your backyard but not your neighbor's," said transportation analyst John Anderson of Greenbriar Equity Group to Bloomberg News in March of 2012. "It's just good luck."[6]

Good luck or good foresight? When Warren is contemplating a deal, he does his homework to understand the industry, the marketplace, the company's competitors, and the business. He knows cost of sales, cost of goods sold, depreciation, asset base, network, and what the Q factor is inside the business, but most important, he understands the trigger points of how the company generates revenue and what its cost structures are.

So when Warren decides to make a megadeal, he does not hesitate. That's why in 2009, a man worth about $44 billion was willing to spend $26.5 billion to acquire the 77.5 percent of BNSF that he did not already own. Warren simply called it "the most important purchase Berkshire ever made."[7]

On Hunting Elephants

When you are going to eat an elephant, don't nibble; jump in and get the deal done. If Warren decides to strike, he doesn't strike with half measures. The BNSF deal was just peanuts for Warren. In 2010, he had almost $40 billion, and he wanted to spend it. The "elephant gun is reloaded, and my trigger finger is itchy," he said in his annual letter to shareholders. However, when Warren hunts elephants, it is just him, Charlie Munger, and a checkbook the size of Fort Knox. You don't have that. You need a team to jump in and get the deal done.

You surely understand by now that your next big deal is going to take more people than just you. You simply can't do this alone. It's too big, too complex, and too important to you and your company.

The biggest thing your team can do for you and your next big deal is to take fear off the table. Let us look at ways for you to make that happen.

===== WARREN WAY 16 =====

Hunting Big Deals

Author Janet Lowe reported in *Warren Buffett Speaks* that on a 2002 trip to Britain, Buffett told the U.K. *Sunday Telegraph* that he was looking for a "big deal" in that country. "We are hunting elephant.... We have got an elephant gun and it's loaded."

You need different eyes, better eyes, and different voices helping you.

Different eyes indicates the advantage of having a group of people brainstorm your ideas and your presentations. Each member of your team sees things in an individual way, and therefore each can pinpoint problems with or suggest added benefits to your solution. As a result, your next Warren Buffett kind of deal benefits from having creativity, imagination, and energy that it might not otherwise have had.

Better eyes, of course, indicates that many times the different eyes see angles or hidden aspects in ways that greatly magnify the power of your solution.

Different voices indicates the advantage of having many contributions to the drafting of your presentations and written documents. Different voices also help in arriving at an overall tone for your hunt. And it probably goes without saying that some of these voices will arrive at a much better way to express something than you would have thought of alone.

Many dealmakers with whom we work have problems with the idea of needing a team. So let us address that directly before we go any further.

This is in no way a reflection on your deal-making abilities. In fact, you'll find that hunting your next big deal—even with a team— will test your salesmanship beyond any previous tests. One of the biggest satisfactions of hunting your elephant-size deal is that you'll find yourself using new techniques and coming up with solutions in new ways.

You Are Not Your Prospect's Only Choice

When they're making a huge deal, like your next big Warren Buffett deal, prospects are extremely fearful of making a *big* mistake. Instead of taking the chance that comes with your solution to their problem, the prospect has other choices, all of them safer than you.

1. *Do nothing.* "If it ain't broke, don't fix it."
2. *Take your suggestions and do it internally.* Assign the solution to some current employees. "The devil you know..."
3. *Find a really cheap alternative to you.* "But it was almost free."
4. *Hire the biggest company in your industry.* "Big brands are safer."

As a single salesperson, you can't deal successfully with your prospect's fears or the intricacies of the deal. You need people with you who have the expertise to provide the rational, accurate, detailed answers that can drive the fear away and who can help you handle the responsibilities involved in your next big Warren Buffett–style deal.

So let's find those people, both within and outside your company.

Look Within Your Company

We'll start by looking at what is closest to you, your company. Let's look at four different categories of people:

1. Subject-matter experts
2. Your executives
3. Your current and former clients
4. Others

Subject-matter experts in your company can be pivotal in eliminating your prospects' fears.

Here's a possible scenario. You're selling a solution to your prospect's biggest problem: cutting expenses. You've figured out a way to help your prospect eliminate five steps from a twelve-step process. Your solution involves some outsourcing, some system changes, and a serious reconfiguration of personnel.

You're promising your prospect a return on investment within three months, plus your solution will reduce operating costs year after year and raise market share.

You're going into a meeting where your prospect has gathered people from several departments to hear your proposal. All these departments will be directly involved in carrying out your solution, and their representatives are there to question you. Their questions are given in the following table.

DEPARTMENT	QUESTION
Financial	*How exactly did you arrive at your figures guaranteeing ROI in three months, and how can you possibly guarantee a reduction in operating costs year after year?*
Operations	*How can we maintain quality when we're reducing a twelve-step process to seven steps?*
Human resources	*How will we maintain employee morale with all this shifting of positions?*
Information technology	*How will this system interface with all our other systems?*
Public relations	*How do we keep from appearing heartless and ruthless when news of this gets out?*
Legal	*Can you explain how you will resolve the legal complications involved in this solution?*

Why are all those people at the meeting? Because they, and their CEO, are afraid. Your solution has filled them with fear. Remember, you have already crossed the threshold of interest. That is what got everyone into the room. However, interest and excitement are not the drivers of purchase. Fear is.

They love all the positive elements of your solution, but all their questions have, as an underlying basis, great fear.

1. Fear over the accuracy of your numbers and flaws in your financial hypotheses
2. Fear over losing quality and thus losing customers

3. Fear over employee discontent causing disruptions and turnovers

4. Fear of the extra work involved in dealing with new systems that require time and money

5. Fear of a public relations disaster

6. Fear of lawsuits

Notice the extreme difference in viewpoint and language in these issues. Each of these questions requires an individual on your team who can see (*better eyes*) the issue from the viewpoint of the questioner and answer (*better voice*) it in terms that will resonate with the department head who is asking the question.

Any *one* of these fears, if unresolved, can destroy your deal. But how can that be? You've put together 90 percent of your solution, and you are running along just fine. But the remaining small percentage—anticipating and eliminating fears—can and will defeat you.

Just imagine a lawyer leaning forward across the table and saying, "Well, I have some real problems with this. You're going to have dozens of employee discrimination lawsuits unless you're very careful with exactly how this is handled. Given what I've heard so far, my vote would be no." Your solution will probably die right there.

The Great Power of the Veto

Although the one person who can say yes to a deal is extremely important, even more important are all those who can say no. Sometimes we skew our presentations too much toward convincing just one person to say yes.

The veto power involved here is actually tiny, but it takes only one person. The CEO may love your solution, but if one of the people from his team who is involved (remember that the CEO invited these people into the discussion) says no, the odds that you won't be successful are overwhelming.

Why should this be? Because you're proposing a solution that has wide impact throughout a division, a department, or the company. It's change on a big scale. Change potentially means disruption, conflict, additional work, and possible failure. Some people believe it's better to stay with what is known and safe.

Your prospects will keep a system that loses money rather than go with a new one that is demonstrably better if someone on the team convinces them to be very afraid of what you're proposing.

So never make the mistake of thinking, "It's no big thing if that one person isn't convinced that this is a good idea." That one person could be the one who kills your deal.

Accept the fact that the members of the prospect's team have, as their primary mission, the chance to say no. Then work to find ways to eliminate that veto.

How Do You Eliminate the Fear?

You eliminate the fear by including on your team the people from your company who are best equipped to give in-depth answers to all the questions that are being raised. You take your subject-matter experts with you. They will be able to understand the issues from all the different viewpoints (eyes), use the language their counterparts use, and explain all the ins and outs of all the details (voice). Your financial person talks with the prospect's financial person, your operations person with the prospect's operations person, and so on.

In the case mentioned earlier involving the lawyer, your human resources person will have recognized the issues early on, sought advice, and be able to say, "We've talked with our attorneys, and we've developed a plan with them that takes all legal concerns into consideration. Let me tell you about it." Although you could also talk about this plan, your prospect won't have the same confidence in your answers that he will have in your human resources person's answers. Why not? You don't have the correct eyes or voice. The HR person does.

Eliminating the fear involves a large amount of specificity. Most often, a question will take the following form, "What will you do when such and such happens?" To answer that question successfully, you need to talk with knowledge, confidence, and depth about a number of different areas. And quite frankly, that's not your job. It's the job of your subject-matter experts. Let them do it.

Some Subject-Matter Experts May Drag Their Feet

Some subject-matter experts have the unfortunate viewpoint that they shouldn't be involved in any sales activity because, "That's not my job. My job is finance, not sales." They believe that sales are the job of the sales department. There are at least three problems with that mentality:

1. Your next Warren Buffett deal will be so big that it will involve those same subject-matter experts on a daily basis during implementation. It's in their best interests to be certain that you aren't selling something they can't deliver.
2. The good old days of "silo" management and thinking are gone. The subject-matter experts' future rises and falls with the entire company's future.
3. You can't make a deal of this size without them. They are crucial to your success.

Just remember that you may have to do a major selling pitch to get some subject matter-experts involved. They have to understand not only that this deal is great for the company but, even more important, that it'll be a big win for them and their department.

Be sure to eliminate their fears about even being part of your next Warren Buffett kind of deal when you make your recruitment pitch.

Your executive (CEO or other high-level executive) always presents a unique kind of issue when it comes to landing your next big Warren Buffett–style deal. It's difficult to hit on the exact right amount of participation by that person. However, that balance can be found if the following statements are true:

1. Your executive is fully behind your landing your next big deal and your method for doing it.
2. Your executive is spoken to in person only to eliminate fear.
3. Your executive meets with you in private to give her viewpoint and to suggest appropriate language.

If you both agree on these statements, you can resolve any issue that might arise.

Tip: Never Use Your CEO as the Ultimate Negotiator of Price

The CEO's role in setting price is behind the scenes, not in front of the prospect.

Price decisions need to be made before or after the meeting. They are relayed to prospects by the CEO only when she is trying to eliminate fear by demonstrating personal commitment.

Using your CEO as the price negotiator during in-person visits weakens the team and guarantees future difficulties in client management.

Your executive will be involved to show his support for your next big Warren kind of deal and to eliminate any fears that he can resolve. The most obvious of these fears is prospects' fear that your company won't fully back you in implementing your Warren-style deal. The prospect may be imagining that you will get involved in the next big deal and that others will have too much other work to do. The feared result is that implementation won't be fully realized.

Since your solution is likely to result in widespread change within the prospect's company, this is not an unfounded fear. It is very real. You may have to use many different devices to eliminate this fear, but your executive's personal commitment would certainly be a part of these devices.

Finishing Off the Elephant

One of the biggest fears that prospects usually have is a quite simple question: "How do we get started?" They're now poised at the end of a cliff and next to a deep chasm. They can see the other side and the implementation of your solution.

But between now and then, there is a huge chasm that they cannot cross in their imagination. This, of course, makes them very afraid. You have to help them cross the chasm of change.

Building a bridge across the chasm for them will eliminate that gigantic fear and show them your competence, your ability to anticipate and strategize, and your willingness to share a little of the load of transition.

=== WARREN WAY 52 ===

Deals Can Take Time

"No matter how great the talent or efforts, some things just take time. You can't produce a baby in one month by getting nine women pregnant."

What the prospects want to know is, "What happens between now and then?" And you have to be prepared to answer completely and with confidence.

"Trust us. It'll be done," won't eliminate any fear.

Your deals are probably going to take longer than Warren's do. So let's look at how you can develop your transition map:

1. *Start with the question.* What will we do today or tomorrow to move this forward? And you take it from there.

2. *Name and define clearly each step* that you will take between now and full implementation. Think of everything. Nothing is too trivial to be included.

- Actions to be taken
- People from both companies to be involved
- Training that will be needed
- Person(s) from your company who are responsible for each step
- Timeline for each step
- Individual to contact in case the prospect has questions

3. *Set a regular communication schedule* with the prospects to keep them fully informed.

4. *Establish milestones with key performance indicators* so that you and the prospects can discuss how everything is going. Define your results threshold for rollout up front. At each step, what results do you need to produce and what results do your prospects need to see so that you can move seamlessly through the steps?

5. *Establish partial completion points:* the 30 percent completion point, the 50 percent completion point, and so on.

6. *Establish an ROI schedule* that can be used to evaluate the deal.

This transition map is essential when you're hunting your elephant-size deal. Since this is such a large deal and since prospects are fearful, sometimes they will say, "Let's try a little and see how that works." Don't fall into that trap.

We recently worked with a company in the far Northwest. It would sell an initial implementation—fairly complex engineering sales—and it would sell almost any volume it could get.

The volume that would allow the company to work out the kinks, really engineer the product, and work through the implementation was 10,000 units. But the salespeople were allowed to go out and sell 5,000 units.

Well, do you want to know what the first 5,000 units looked like? A mess.

During the implementation of the first 5,000 units, the company was just getting the supply chain management right. It was working through the orientation of parts in the inline manufacturing process. The first 5,000 units is where all the hard, bumpy work gets done. If the prospects really wanted to know what the future would look like working with that company, the best vantage point would be to view it during the implementation of the *second* 5,000 units.

If you let yourself get caught in the "try it and see how it goes" trap, you won't have made the next big deal you wanted to make, and your prospects will be disappointed with the results. Chances are you'll lose the deal entirely.

Selling 5,000 when you know that the only way for prospects to really understand your value proposition is to buy 10,000 will not get you your elephant deal. If the prospect isn't interested in buying your entire deal, you need to find other prospects that will be. Don't sell yourself short.

Buffett Bonus | People Make the Difference

Buffett is a shrewd judge of character and a student of human relations. "Somebody once said that in looking for people to hire, you look for three qualities: integrity, intelligence and energy," Buffett told the *Omaha World Herald*, long before he purchased the newspaper in 2011. "And if they don't have the first, the other two will kill you." When he buys a company, Buffett tries to avoid managerial changes. In fact, he insists that the businesses come with a competent management team already in place. He requires key managers to write a letter saying whom they would recommend to replace them if they should die. Who better to be a manager than a person who was personally chosen by the manager who's currently running the show? But Buffett knows that judging humans is imperfect at best. "There is no way to eliminate the possibility of error when judging humans."

A Little Help
Goes a Long Way

W ARREN SEES nothing wrong with asking for a little help from his business buddies.

When Warren made the deal to acquire furniture giant RC Willey in 1995, he asked CEO Bill Child if there were any other furniture industry standouts that he recommended. Star Furniture of Houston was at the top of the list. Star operated 12 stores—10 in Houston and 1 each in Austin and Bryan—and was planning to move into San Antonio as well.

But time went by, and there seemed to be no indication that the company was available. Then Melvyn Wolff, the longtime controlling shareholder and CEO of Star Furniture of Houston, decided that he wanted to talk to Warren. He asked Bob Denham of Salomon to set up a sit-down with Warren two days before the 1997 Berkshire Hathaway annual meeting.

At Warren's invitation, Wolff stayed for the annual meeting and spent his time in Omaha confirming his positive feelings about Berkshire. That's easy to do at a Berkshire annual meeting, which has been called "Woodstock for capitalists." Meanwhile, Warren looked at Star's financials and liked what he saw.

The deal was quickly made in typical Warren fashion. A few days later, Wolff and Warren met in New York and made a deal in a single two-hour session. As was the case with Nebraska Furniture Mart and RC Willey, Warren felt that he had no need to check leases, work out employment contracts, or do other due diligence. "I knew I was dealing with a man of integrity and that's what counted," said Warren in the 1997 annual report.

"Here's a story illustrating what Melvyn and [his wife] Shirley are like: When they told their associates of the sale, they also announced that Star would make large, special payments to those who had helped them succeed—and then defined that group as everyone in the business," added Warren. "Under the terms of our deal, it was Melvyn and Shirley's money, not ours, that funded this distribution. Charlie [Munger] and I love it when we become partners with people who behave like that."

Recruit Clients to Help

As seen on the TV game show *Who Wants to Be a Millionaire?* sometimes it really does pays to phone a friend.

Think about the next Warren Buffett deal you want to make. The CEO of your prospective deal will have fears about your solution that are perhaps hers alone. An excellent way for you to alleviate those fears is by giving her a chance to talk with another person in her position who's happy with your work.

As you've read through this book, perhaps you've occasionally had mental questions about the efficacy of what you were reading. When, a few pages later, you read a story about one of our clients who was successful, didn't a great deal of your fear dissipate? This is always true. If we see someone else who is successful, we become much less fearful.

Usually the best method of communication, CEO to CEO, is by phone. You'll have to assess the willingness of both parties to use this approach. Some of your clients might want a list of subjects that can or cannot be discussed. And, of course, no CEO is going to want to give out any proprietary information to a competitor.

That being said, there is still a wealth of information that one CEO can give to another. Here are some examples:

1. What's it like to work with your company?
2. How does your company handle emergencies?
3. Can your company be trusted to deliver what it promises?
4. Does your company stay within schedules?
5. Does your company go beyond the agreed-upon budget?

General or specific questions about your work style are appropriate for any CEO to ask or answer. Always remember that your intent is to eliminate your prospect's fear of working with you.

How can you best use your coworkers to eliminate fear? One of the most effective ways to do that is to exhibit a high quality of excellence every time you "touch" the prospects in any way.

If you show any incompetence in your normal day-to-day dealings with your prospects, they will not trust you to be competent in carrying out your solution.

In a deal of this size, certain roles and responsibilities have to be undertaken, and no one person can perform all of them successfully. Following is a list of four responsibilities that should be distributed.

=== **WARREN WAY 99** ===

Be Honest in Your Deal Making

Buffett told his son Howard: "It takes 20 years to build a reputation and five minutes to ruin it. If you think about that, you'll do things differently."

Please note that this is *not* a list of *people* that you need to have on your team. It's a list of *responsibilities* that, if performed with care and precision, will make your process run smoothly.

1. *The technician.* This person provides the necessary language, history, and context to the discussion as it relates to the prospect's

company and its potential purchase from your company. You have to eliminate the fear that comes from your prospect's thinking that his company is unique and that "you just don't understand how things work here." Be certain to show that you do understand.

2. *The flow.* This person gets the sense of the prospect's people and keeps the sales process communication moving. This is the person who, with ease, checks in now and then with people in the prospect company to see "how things are going." She also oversees the access of others in your company to the prospect company, so that no one will ever give out conflicting information, mispronounce the CEO's name, or do anything else that can stall your process. She eliminates your prospect's fear that "you don't have your act together."

3. *The strategist.* This person handles people, motivations, approaches, and structure for the meetings, sales calls, and overall pitch. This person determines the purposes and desired outcomes for all meetings, selects the most appropriate people to be in attendance, outlines how the pitch will be made, and handles strategic issues as they present themselves. He is the one who decides exactly what fear will be eliminated by whom.

4. *The host.* This person oversees every part of an official visit to your company. If part of your strategy requires your prospect to visit your workplace, you want someone to be responsible for every minute of that prospect's day with you. If your entryway has peeling paint, repaint it. If your prospect will be talking with various people, prepare them for that exchange beforehand. Don't leave anything to chance. You want to eliminate any possible fear that you "appear not to care."

You will undoubtedly have other roles and responsibilities related to other fears. You may have people who are capable of playing more than one role on your team, but it's more than likely that you won't have "the complete package" in one person. Hardly anyone ever does, and that is OK.

Look Outside Your Company

Again we start with your prospect's deal-making fears. Suppose one fear is this: *you don't have enough capacity to handle this deal—money, facilities, and resources.*

If you have identified this as a fear that your prospects are apt to have, then you should begin thinking about the people you want on your team. Who can eliminate this particular fear? Whom do you know who can vividly show your capability in the areas of money, facilities, and resources?

Maybe you're thinking, "Well, if I could take *anybody* I wanted with me to a presentation, I'd take my banker, my architect, and my audiovisual person. And maybe my IT guy. But I can't do that."

=== **WARREN WAY 40** ===

Invest in the Company That You Keep.

"It's better to hang out with people better than you. Pick out associates whose behavior is better than yours and you'll drift in that direction."

Who said? Guess what? There's good news. *You can take anyone you want to a presentation.* Yes, that's right. You can take anyone and everyone. Take the people who will eliminate the fear.

But, conventional wisdom says:

1. You have to use only salespeople. They're the most important part of the team.
2. You have to use only people from your company. You don't want others to know what you're doing.
3. You have to use only people from your industry. People from other industries won't know what you're talking about.

Well, conventional wisdom is wrong, wrong, and wrong. You can and must use the people who can best take fear off the table, no matter who they might be. And very often, they are not salespeople—or even people in your industry.

No one in the entire world can better speak about your capacity in the area of money than your banker.

You can tell the prospect that you have great financial assets available to you, and you can bring statement and graphs to prove it. Remember your *better eyes* and *better voices*.

But imagine that you have your banker there, and she looks the prospect in the eye and says, "I can vouch for the financial capacity of this company to do this deal. I meet with _____ (that's you) and his financial people every month to review their assets and liabilities. We have a financial strategic plan, and this deal fits right in there. It can be accomplished with little or no strain on the company's finances, budgets, or other plans for the future."

Your architect, your audiovisual person, and your IT person can all do the same type of thing. Because they know the territory thoroughly and can talk the talk, they can take away the prospect's fear in 15 minutes, something that you wouldn't be able to do in a half-day session.

Weird but True

Would prospects think you might overstate your own financial capacity in order to get the deal?

Yes, they would.

But would they think your banker would take the time to come to the meeting and lie about your financial capacity?

No, they wouldn't.

Why would people from outside your company help you in winning your next big deal? There are probably as many reasons as there are people. But let's look at three:

1. *Being asked.* They've never been asked before. Someone did a survey of wealthy people, asking whether they had made donations

to not-for-profit organizations, and if not, why not. The number one reason for not giving was that they hadn't been asked to do so. For many people, just being asked to do something out of the ordinary carries a lot of satisfaction.

2. *Broadening their horizons.* They're meeting people whom they've not met before in a setting that is probably new to them. It's a different world from the one they usually live in, and that's exciting.

3. *Local emphasis.* If you and your company do well, the entire community benefits, including them. You might bring a direct benefit to your local bank or your local architect, making them very glad to help you land your deal. Besides, if you're already a customer, they want to keep you. If you're not, they want to make you one.

If you're running a business with few employees, you'll especially need to include people from outside your company on your team. Bring all the right people, even if you use contractors. Perhaps you contract out all your payroll, HR, accounting, audiovisual development, or anything else. You should include the people who actually do this work in your team when they're needed.

Just remember that your basic issue is to eliminate fears. Wherever your contract employees can do that, they should be included.

Remember, don't nibble on the elephant. Some of the most important decisions you will make in hunting your next big deal are your decisions about who should be on your team. *You want people who can help eliminate your prospect's fears.* That's the major responsibility of your team. But you also want those who see situations and people in different ways from you and who can talk about issues in the language of your prospect's buying team members.

Don't let yourself get stuck in outdated conventional wisdom patterns about who "should" be on your team.

Keep an open mind and select the best people possible, whether or not they're in your industry or your company.

Buffett Bonus | Find the Right Help

Asking the right people to help manage his businesses is a secret of Warren Buffett's success. In the foreword to the book *Beating the Odds*, by Leonard Goldenson, Buffett summed up his management philosophy: "Business management can be viewed as a three-act play—the dream, the execution, and the passing of the baton." When picking business partners to manage a business, he looks for people he can depend on. He wants people who do not let their egos get in the way and are perfectly willing to let others take the credit. He also thinks managers should be left to make their own decisions. He is quoted making another baseball analogy by Peter Lynch in *One Up On Wall Street*: "At Berkshire we don't tell .400 hitters how to swing."

Victory Favors the Ready

IN THE early 1980s, Rose Blumkin and her son Louie regularly spurned offers to sell their Nebraska Furniture Mart, by then the largest furniture store in North America. Housed under one roof, the multiacre store sold more than $100 million of furniture a year.

One of the offers they had summarily dismissed had come from Warren, who wanted to make a deal to add the legendary retailer to the Berkshire Hathaway family. The fact that the store sold ten times the volume of stores of similar size had not escaped his notice.

A Jewish immigrant who had escaped the brutality of czarist pogroms and the Russian Revolution, Rose (known to all as Mrs. B) had founded the store in an Omaha basement in 1937. "If you have the lowest price, customers will find you at the bottom of a river," she said.

Her ruthless belief in selling at tiny margins created rough going early on. Furniture manufacturers boycotted Mrs. B at the urging of local competitors, who enjoyed operating at higher markups. Traveling by train to Kansas City, Chicago, and New York, she became a furniture bootlegger, a proficient bargain hunter who bought from large furniture stores at 5 percent over their cost and still made a profit using her low-markup sales strategy.

Her son Louie Blumkin, a World War II veteran, joined his mother in the business in 1946 and contributed immeasurably to the growth and success of Nebraska Furniture Mart. Even a devastating tornado in 1975 caused only a minor setback in the growth of the business. Despite millions of dollars in damage to the store, Mrs. B and her son simply rebuilt it bigger and better.

In 1983, Warren heard that the Blumkin family was negotiating to sell to a company in Hamburg, Germany, that operated the largest furniture store in the world. Warren sprang into action.

By then, most of the day-to-day operations had been turned over to Louie Blumkin. Warren struck up a relationship with Louie, who soon said to Warren, "You should meet my sons, Ron and Irv, who'll be running the store someday."

Warren was impressed with the success, business savvy, and honest dealings of the Blumkins. He responded with similar honesty, sending Louie Blumkin a letter outlining both the pros and the cons of selling to Berkshire.

According to Buffett biographer Alice Schroeder, the letter made points along the following lines:

> They could sell to another furniture company, he wrote, or to somebody in a similar business. But "such a buyer—no matter what promises are made—usually will have managers who feel they know how to run your business operations, and sooner or later, will want to get into hands-on activity." Then there is "the financial maneuverer, usually operating on large amounts of borrowed money, who plans to resell either to the public or to another corporation as soon as the time is favorable," he wrote. "If the sellers' business represents the creative work of a lifetime and remains an integral part of the personality and sense of being, both types of buyers have serious flaws. Any buyer will tell you that he needs you and, if he has any brains, he most certainly needs you. But a great many, for the reasons mentioned above, don't subsequently behave in that manner. We will behave exactly as promised, both because we have so promised, and because we need to."[8]

Warren explained that he wanted and needed the Blumkins to stay on as his partners. In addition, he had something else to offer: he was from Omaha, not Germany. Selling to Germans was repulsive to Mrs. B, although they offered $35 million more than Warren was offering.

Then came the clincher: "I don't even want to take inventory," Warren said. "I'll take your word, Mrs. B, whatever you say you got."

To seal the deal, Warren visited the 89-year-old Rose on her three-wheeled golf cart at the store. Warren and Mrs. B used a simple handshake to seal the purchase of 90 percent of the business for $55 million. The handshake and simple two-page written agreement were all that were required—no audit of the store's books, no inventory of its merchandise. (Soon after, Berkshire auditors conducted Nebraska Furniture Mart's first inventory and found that the store was actually worth $85 million.)

After the deal was done, Warren said: "Mrs. B, I've got to tell you something. It's my birthday today." That day he turned 53.

Rose Blumkin replied: "You bought an oil well on your birthday."

Try These Maneuvers

You'll want to spend many hours with your team in maneuvers, preparing for the presentations to be made in front of the prospects. There is no doubt that you will spend more time in preparing than you will in the actual presentation. But it's time that is extremely well spent and vital for your success.

Don't limit your preparation to thinking about *what you should say or do*, then consider yourself ready for your meeting. That's a genuinely disastrous way to prepare, and it won't get you the success you want.

Practice the actual saying and doing. Lead your team members through their parts in the presentation, and make certain they know how to react appropriately to any kind of interruption or question.

========= WARREN WAY 46 =========

Be Ready, but Don't Force Deals

"You do things when the opportunities come along. I've had periods in my life when I've had a bundle of opportunities come along, and I've had long dry spells. If I get an idea next week, I'll do something. If not, I won't do a damn thing."

These maneuvers have worked time after time for my clients. Using the maneuvers gives them a wonderful sense of freedom and control during the process. And actually saying and doing makes them very successful in their hunts.

Murder Boards and Hot Washes

In the military academies, seniors preparing for their oral exams use two key processes for preparation and improvement called murder boards and hot washes. These processes work as well in sales as they do in the military. They will increase your sales effectiveness by huge multiples if you include them in your sales process.

Murder Boards

A murder board is a committee of selected peers and teachers that prepares a student for oral exams by posing anticipated questions to the student and then providing a critique of the answers. This same process is now used by politicians who are preparing for debates, and we hope you will use it in preparing for key presentations. (Warren has his own version of a murder board: his partner and vice chairman, Charlie Munger.)

To get the full value of the murder board process, you need the following components:

1. *Really smart people.* The people on the board should be knowl-edgeable about your business, your industry, your competitors, and the prospect.

2. *Enough time.* The murder board process will take twice as long as the presentation itself, and then some. To be successful, you'll need to go through the presentation from start to finish without sidebar interruptions. Then you'll have an aggressive question-and-answer period from your murder board, designed to challenge you and help you shape your presentation as well as your answers.

3. *Your full pitch team.* Include the people who are going to be doing the pitch—*all of them.* The absence of just one person during the murder board session can create a damaging dynamic in the fol-lowing actual presentation.

You're doing this process with the intention of sharpening yourself, and your team, up to a razor level so that you can deliver a fantastic and successful presentation. Right? So don't do it halfheartedly

An old poker saying is: "You don't play your cards, you play every-body else's." To win the pitch, keep this in mind. Prepare for what the other people going to say as much as you rehearse what you will say.

To get the most out of your murder board, follow this framework:

1. *Assign the voices.* You probably know the people to whom you will be pitching. For this reason, assign those people's perspectives and personas to members of your murder board. This can be funny, but that's not the point. The real issue is that you want finance ques-tions from the finance guy, technical questions from the tech person, and so on. This also allows your murder board participants to be more focused in their listening and their challenges.

2. *Bucket the questions.* You need to get the questions into con-text. It's not helpful to your cause if you just get random questions. Although that may be what you actually anticipate getting at the meeting, in rehearsal, it is more helpful in developing consistent and

coherent answers if you have grouped the questions. We recommend the inclusion of these categories of questions, but you should feel free to add and edit your categories:

- *Compare and contrast.* These are questions asking you to speak about your company in relationship to your competitors.
- *Why.* Examples include: "Why should we hire your company?" and "Why did you choose to use that technology?" These are intentionally challenging because the implication is that another option is better or is one that the prospect prefers. That may not be the case, but the question does challenge your approach.
- *Implementation.* These are nuts-and-bolts questions about working together. Who? How? When? Using what process? Address them all.

3. Check your blind spots. A good murder board member will be looking for those areas that are underrepresented or missing in your solution or presentation. These underrepresented areas need to be determined during the preparation so that special attention can be paid to them.

4. Identify your known vulnerabilities. When you have done a few presentations, you will become very familiar with the areas in your business that are weak. It may be your size, your technology, your financial strength, or other concerns. These are your weak spots. Your strategy is to craft airtight answers to questions in these areas and rehearse them. This is particularly important to ensure great use of your murder board in the preparation process.

5. Shoot for three. On the key areas, murder board members need to push three questions deep into each area. The follow-up questions are more important than the initial questions. Your prospect will dig, so your murder board needs to dig, too.

6. Record the session. Don't trust your notes or your memory. Great things come out of these sessions, and you want to make certain to get them all. An audio recording is fine—the equipment is cheap. A video recording is better yet if you can make one. The technology is not as important as the ability to review the answers, capturing the best ones and enabling you to improve the weak ones.

We recommend that you do the murder board exercise *within 48 to 72 hours of your presentation.* This gives you enough time to practice and revise, but not so much time that you second-guess and forget.

Hot Washes

After the military academy exams, students either reconvene their murder boards or use other advisors and mentors to do a thorough review of the exam called a hot wash. This is to make certain that the lessons were learned. Again, politicians now use this approach so that they can improve from one debate or presentation to the next.

This process is a review seeking to identify two to five key lessons for the future. In doing a hot wash, the process should be relatively quick and surgical in its approach.

Here is the way in which the conversation should be structured:

1. *What parts of the process worked?* A presentation starts at the lobby and ends when you get in the car after it is over. There is a process in the middle—how you enter the room, where you sit, how you present, who presents in what order, how you handle questions and answers, and so on. Without focusing on the content, ask questions about process and score each of the steps in terms of its successfulness.

2. *What content worked?* You need to capture the language, the content, and the tools used that the presenting team or person felt worked. Focus on this question in the dialogue, "What behavior did you see from the prospect that made you feel that this element worked?"

3. *What relationships worked?* Often there are connections made between people in the session. Possibly it is because of a shared background in education or where they grew up. It could be because of a well-received answer to a question. Whatever the cause, relation-ships are forming and possibly improving during the presentation. Name them.

4. *Reverse the field.* Now cover the three areas just discussed with the reverse mentality—focus on what didn't work. Be honest and get it out on the table.

5. *What will we change?* Focus on the two or three important aspects that you will structurally change in your approach. You may decide that a particular picture is too dark for the PowerPoint, but that's not what we are really talking about here. You are looking for the more important things that will make a difference in all your presentations going forward.

6. *What will we do exactly the same?* Focus on the substantial two to three changes that you will make in the future.

7. You are looking for the high-leverage things you did in this pre-sentation that you want to make a part of your permanent arsenal. Focus on the substantial two to three changes that you will make in the future.

To this day, we use murder boards and hot washes with sales teams we are coaching on their biggest deals. They increase confidence and force learning for real improvement. Being prepared doesn't guaran-tee a deal, but it sure helps improve the odds.

Buffett Bonus | Also Be Ready to Know the Deals to Avoid

You will do better by avoiding dragons than by slaying them, advises Buffett. The people and the economics of the deal have to make sense. Buffett says, "Good jockeys will do well on good horses, but not on broken-down nags." Hard work and integrity do not cure everything. He adds: "I've said many times that when a management with a reputation for brilliance tackles a business with a reputation for bad economics, it is the reputation of the business that remains intact. I just wish I hadn't been so energetic in creating examples. My behavior has matched that admitted by Mae West: 'I was Snow White, but I drifted.'"

In 1989, Buffett also said that after 25 years of buying and supervising a wide variety of businesses, Charlie Munger and he had not learned how to solve difficult business problems. "What we have learned is to avoid them. To the extent we have been successful, it is because we concentrated on identifying one-foot hurdles that we could step over rather than because we acquired any ability to clear seven-footers."

LESSON 12

The Why Matters

IN AN unusual strategic disposal, Walmart sold its McLane Company division to Warren in a $1.45 billion deal in 2003. McLane is an example of a firm that didn't really fit as a holding of the giant retailer but was a welcome addition to Warren's collection of companies. But why?

McLane, based in Temple, Texas, was one of the nation's largest wholesale distributors of groceries and nonfood items to convenience stores, drugstores, wholesale clubs, mass merchandisers, quick-service restaurants, theaters, and other establishments. It had been acquired by Walmart back in 1990.

But why would Walmart want to sell? Revenues were not the problem. Prior to the acquisition in 2003, McLane had annual sales of about $22 billion. It was already the largest distributor to convenience stores in the country.

Indeed, for Walmart, selling a piece of itself was a rare event; according to the *New York Times*, one company executive said that he could not recall its having happened before.

Warren's why was easier to grasp. The deal would allow McLane to continue handling distribution for Walmart, but the shift in ownership freed it to pursue distribution contracts with Walmart competitors such as Target and Dollar General, as well as for supermarket chains.

The deal followed Warren's pattern. Warren likes a noncomplex business that is easy to understand. The grocery delivery business fits that description. It is also a business that is unlikely to fundamentally change the way it operates or be threatened by new inventions. Warren likes companies that provide people with goods that they are going to continue to need in good times and bad. Obviously, people are going to continue to need groceries.

Burt Flickinger, managing partner with the Strategic Resource Group, a retail consulting firm, called the deal "a real home run for both Walmart and Buffett." It came at a time when $7 billion in food-distribution sales could be in play, depending upon whether Fleming emerged from its Chapter 11 bankruptcy court filing.

Analysts did not expect a culture clash in the transfer from Walmart to Berkshire Hathaway. Both companies drape their competitiveness in a down-home manner. In fact, Warren had even visited Walmart's headquarters in Bentonville, Arkansas, to speak at its Saturday morning meeting for store managers.

Warren understood the why for Walmart: addition by subtraction. He saw the move as Walmart's effort to shed a business in which profits are narrow and prospects seemed dimmer than they had when Walmart purchased it 13 years earlier. With razor-thin operating margins of about 2 percent, and given the economics of convenience stores, McLane was the weakest link at Walmart. Warren understood that it was the lowest-margin business that Walmart had, so taking it out of the portfolio was going to improve Walmart's overall financial returns.

"In the past, some retailers had shunned McLane because it was owned by their major competitor," said Warren in the 2003 letter to shareholders. "Grady Rosier, McLane's superb CEO, has already landed some of these accounts—he was in full stride the day the deal closed—and more will come."

Once Warren understood the why, the deal moved along in typical speedy fashion.

"For several years, I have given my vote to Wal-Mart in the balloting for *Fortune* Magazine's 'Most Admired' list," Warren added.

"Our McLane transaction reinforced my opinion. To make the McLane deal, I had a single meeting of about two hours with Tom Schoewe, Wal-Mart's CFO, and we then shook hands." (He did, however, first call Bentonville.) Twenty-nine days later Wal-Mart had its money. "We did no 'due diligence.' We knew everything would be exactly as Wal-Mart said it would be—and it was."

When You Know the Why, the How Follows

Start with understanding of why a deal makes sense to your prospect. Once you know your prospect's biggest problems, you'll need to find your biggest solution to match. You already know that the solution must solve your prospect's biggest problems, but here are three other questions that you must answer.

Question 1:
Does Your Warren Buffett Deal Show 8 to 14 Percent Improvement for the Prospect, and Is It Credible?

A rule of thumb is to make sure that your solution shows an 8 to 14 percent improvement for your prospect. That may be an improvement in costs, in ramp-up time, in on-schedule installations, or whatever else is a major initiative for your prospect.

If you can't get to 8 percent, your solution won't be considered worth the time. On the other hand, if you go too far beyond 14 percent, your prospect will have trouble believing that your facts are correct, and you'll lose your credibility. There are some exceptions to this rule, but it's a good guideline.

What this means to you is that in order to be considered worth the time and appear credible, you'll have to identify every possible cost that may accrue because of the change you are proposing. The improvement has to be calibrated very closely. You can't just suggest that you think this will be the amount of improvement. You have to show the improvement with numbers. And they must be reasonably accurate.

Question 2:
Are the Warren Buffett Deal Costs for Your Company Reasonable and Doable?

Be detailed in assessing the costs for *your company*. Ask and answer the following kinds of questions before you begin your deal making:

1. Will I have to hire additional personnel?
2. Will I need additional technological equipment?
3. Will I have to travel excessively?
4. How quickly can I do this?
5. How much employee time will this take?
6. Will the CEO need to devote huge blocks of time to this?
7. Will I be able to do this project (and others like it) and still keep my smaller deals going?
8. Is this a sensible long-term solution for my company's problems?

Is Your Company Ready to Make Your Warren Buffett Deal?

You need
1. Strong support from your CEO
2. Desire for rapid, explosive growth
3. Stable financials
4. A flexible sales management structure
5. *Willingness to work through new challenges*

Question 3:
Is Your Solution for Your Warren Buffett Deal Quick?

The intersection of the prospect's pain with the speed of your solution is what we call the pointy end of the spear. It's what gives your solution the power to break through the shield of objections that can surround a deal.

The world has changed so dramatically that whatever you once believed was the normal buying cycle or decision cycle has been altered. We cannot put this more strongly. *If the decision is to be made anytime outside of the next six months, move on to another prospect.* The fact is, executives are making decisions in much tighter time frames and formulating strategies with much shorter-term impacts.

Your next big Warren Buffett–style deal will happen rather quickly once the right elements are lined up with the right people because executives no longer have years to make an impact. For this reason, your solutions, and the issues they address, are all moving faster, so you must stress time and speed in all of your discussions. This also means that if the executive does not see the problem as a top priority to be fixed now, *leave.*

A credible solution that takes a year to implement will not win your Warren Buffett deal. Your prospect's problems are happening *now.* And your prospect wants a solution *now.*

Finding Your Solution

In order to find your solution, you must be able to answer the question, "What does my company do exceptionally well *that no one else can or will do*?" Look through the entire company, not just your sales department.

Your company may have an outstandingly efficient inventory system, an ability to do something that no one else wants to do, or an accounting system that keeps track of things other systems don't. Be sure you know what makes your company stand apart from all the rest.

Be honest in your assessment, and don't let yourself fall back into discussing price, service, or quality. These are managerial-level issues, not C-level issues. And they carry a much smaller price tag than your next big Warren Buffett kind of deal demands.

Finding the solution is a difficult task. So, be sure to involve as many of your colleagues as possible in brainstorming. You may very well have unique systems that are not written down, but that your prospect could use.

Case Study: Crown Partners

Let us give you an example of a company that we worked with: Crown Partners, which sells digital strategy solutions.

When the company's leaders decided to go for their next big deal, they knew that they'd have to sell at a higher level in the prospect company. They knew that their current message of "high quality, high service" would have no traction there. So they decided to translate quality and service into something that was more closely related to their prospect's needs.

They realized that what they did that no one else did was perform excellent work in a short period of time. So to win their next big deal, they went to selling time.

This is how Crown Partners figured it out. They realized that a digital strategy implementation that took an entire year could be done by everyone in the industry. However, an implementation that could be completed in six months was rare. A strategy that could be implemented in three months was unheard of. But that was something that Crown Partners could do very well. So, in essence, they sold time.

The language of this deal became, "If you have a year to get this program implemented, almost any credible company in the industry can probably do the work. If you have six months to get this program implemented, then I can give you a list of four or five companies that can do the work. However, if you need this fixed in fewer than three months, we're really the only choice."

Now, Crown Partners has framed its solution in terms that executives can understand and relate to. And, most important, that executives buy.

Your next big Warren Buffett deal is not about you. It's about your prospects. Once Crown Partners understood that its prospects needed service at a much faster pace than other vendors could offer, and once it realized that this was exactly what it did best, then the company had its next big deal. It sold its rapid implementation ability, and that landed its Warren Buffett kind of deal.

Your big Warren Buffett deal is not about your product or service. It's about your prospects' needs. The Crown Partners example points out the reason why you must think in terms of what your prospects will value, rather than in terms of your product or service. Your next big deal solves problems for the market *that the market values.*

As a dealmaker, it's your job to find out what the market values and be sure that that's what you're selling.

Case Study: Volpi Foods

Here's another example of a great strategy from one of our clients, this one from Volpi Foods. When you sell food, you make a reasonable assumption that flavor is what sells it. When you've made food as a business for 106 years and have sold it on flavor, you are certain that flavor is the difference.

The premier U.S. maker of dried Italian meats—salami, pepperoni, and prosciutto—is Volpi Foods. It has worked on a national basis selling and distributing its products to grocers for 106 years, and it has made a really good business out of it.

However, Volpi wanted to grow by landing much bigger deals. The company had been using the same approach it had used for years: meeting with grocers and prospects, showing its products, and handing out samples. However, this just wasn't working when it came to potential Warren Buffett kinds of deals.

You see, flavor is not a business problem. Volpi's value to its clients had to be measured in another way.

If you look at the list of the top 20 grocers in the country—Walmart, Aldi, Kroger, and so on—none of the top people in their meat departments wakes up in the morning and says to herself, "OMG, what am I going to do about my prosciutto flavor problem?"

The top grocers don't have a prosciutto flavor problem. They have different problems, and that is why the value perspective had to change. Volpi had to speak to its big Warren Buffett deal prospects in the language of problems—through money, time, and risk.

A modern grocer is, in fact, a real estate agent. His job is to get the greatest number of dollars per square foot out of the store that he can.

This means that the ways in which value is measured are no longer freshness, texture, and flavor. For the most part, those are expected.

The measures of value are now the following three things:

D = dollars per square foot in revenue and margin

N = number of units moved per week per peg on the refrigerated case pegboard

S = speed of replacement of revenue when a new product is introduced in place of a previous product

The dirty little secret of all this is that flavor is no longer the first question; it's the last question. Flavor is not a business issue. Of course, the food has to taste good, but taste is just the last hurdle in the discussion.

When Volpi figured this out, the company changed its presentation to its next big deal targets to discuss

1. *Margin per unit opportunity* created by a higher perceived value for the product because of the company's reputation, packaging, and repeat prospects (money).

2. *Packaging and merchandising* that would catch the eyes of consumers and attract them to make early first purchases. This decreased the amount of time it normally takes for a replacement product to achieve the same sales as the previous product (risk and time).

3. *Units per week* sales opportunities because of prepared products and recipes to increase frequency of use and repeat purchases (money and time).

4. *Case studies* of other grocers who had achieved results in each area (money, time, and risk).

Once Volpi changed its sales approach, the next big deals rolled out faster and broader.

Volpi brought its prospects new ideas on how to work together on other challenges that they had in their meat area, then in their wine and cheese area, and so on. As a result, Volpi's value changed from that of a food maker and vendor to that of a solution provider.

In many cases, Volpi meats were in the stores before their samples had even been tasted. It's easy to understand why—Volpi was solving a different problem and providing a different value from prosciutto flavor.

Think of it this way.

If you sell T-shirts to retailers and your typical order is for 1,000 shirts, you know how to get size, color, and packaging right.

However, if you want to sell an order for 300,000 shirts, the scope of the problem has just changed. You now have to provide supply chain management, logistics, and a possible returns mechanism that can't be managed out of your garage. The prospect will expect you to stress your performance of these services, not size, color, or packaging.

In other words, your ability to make good shirts just became secondary to those other issues in your conversation with the prospect.

Think of this in terms of "what you sell" and "what your next big deal buys." In your next big Warren Buffett deal, what you sell as a product or service becomes secondary to all the other issues involved in your next big deal.

Discovering what your prospects need is one of the most important activities you can undertake in your quest for your next big Warren Buffett deal. When you begin a major account hunt with only the idea of what you sell, you are not sufficiently armed for the endeavor ahead of you.

You are starting the discussion from one point of view, and your prospects are responding from a totally different one. That's why their buying decisions seem so incomprehensible—because you and they aren't talking the same language.

Fight for Your Why

You lost the deal. The prospect went with the do nothing choice or with another vendor. You are now out time, energy, and a lot of money. I guess that's the way it goes… it's a numbers game, anyway… we learned a lot… really? *No. No. No!* Not without a fight.

How do you fight after the award goes to someone else? Well, you don't play dirty because you want to preserve your relationships and your reputation. But that doesn't mean that you play fair, either. Here are some strategies:

1. *Mafia offer.* Make the prospect an offer she can't refuse. This can come in the form of price, speed, service, or guarantee. This offer has to be made to the highest-level person in the prospect's group, and it has to be made directly. You also have to be prepared to answer the hard question, "If you were willing to make this offer, why wasn't it in your solution?" We have seen a lot of deals won after the award as the result of a Mafia offer.

2. *Split the pie.* Fight for a smaller deal inside of the larger opportunity. The approach to the prospects is straightforward: "You should give yourself two companies to work with so that you can get the best performance from each of them as they compete." You want to set a floor for the size of the smaller part you would take. We use a 30 percent rule of thumb.

3. *The surge.* This is a blitzkrieg approach. You throw everything you have at the prospect's group. Have new closing pitchers called in. Have each of your peer-to-peer players from your company call his counterparts at the prospect company. The appeal is simple: "We appreciate being considered. We are grateful for your time. We are disappointed and a little confused because we felt there was a strong connection between our two companies. What can we do to bring this deal back around?" Your prospect will get it immediately. It knows that you are pushing to win the business. But there is a long distance between "award" and "contract," and you want to be foremost in the prospect's mind as its people go through the challenges of getting a contract signed.

4. *Trip switch.* This appeal is to the senior person in the prospect's group. The approach is that of laying out a challenge: "If the implementation of this deal with our competitor doesn't achieve this performance level milestone by this date, we are willing to pick up the agreement at that time and get you your results." Your prospect will remember this clearly and mentally label it "ace in the hole." You will have distinguished yourself as the fail-safe option.

There really is a long road between making the deal and signing the contract. It is your job to be on that road at every turn. Closing is not done at a certain moment in time. It's part of a longer process that must be managed carefully every step of the way to ensure that the closing is successful. Remember, if the why is strong enough, you will find the how.

=== WARREN WISDOM 77 ===

You Can't Hurry Love or Deals

From *The Essays of Warren Buffett:* "In the search, we adopt the same attitude one might find appropriate in looking for a spouse: It pays to be active, interested, and open-minded, but it does not pay to be in a hurry."

Buffett Bonus | On Screening Deals

Every deal must pencil out in advance. You should be able to explain to others why you are making the deals you are making. The best way to do this is to have a deal filter that you apply to test each deal from the outset. From *The Essays of Warren Buffett:* "Charlie [Munger] and I frequently get approached about acquisitions that don't come close to meeting our tests: We've found that if you advertise an interest in buying collies, a lot of people will call hoping to sell you their cocker spaniels. A line from a country song expresses our feeling about new ventures, turnarounds, or auction-like sales: 'When the phone don't ring, you'll know it's me.'"

LESSON 13

Expect the Unexpected

WHILE THE investment world was high on high-tech stocks at the turn of the millennium, Warren was busy buying construction-related companies. The unexpected can befall even Warren.

In 2000, Warren entered the building-products business, acquiring brick maker Acme Building Brands of Texas and paint maker Benjamin Moore & Co. of New Jersey. Then in 2001, Berkshire bought Shaw Industries, a Georgia company known as the world's largest maker of carpet and laminate flooring.

In 2001, Warren acquired even more building-products companies, including insulation maker Johns Manville and MiTek Inc., which is into engineered connector products such as building trusses.

This was quite a profitable move until the housing bubble burst in 2008.

Two years later, Warren said, "A housing recovery will probably begin within a year or so." He admits that he was dead wrong.

"We have five businesses whose results are significantly influenced by housing activity. The connection is direct at Clayton Homes, which is the largest producer of homes in the country, accounting for about 7 percent of those constructed during 2011. Additionally, Acme Brick, Shaw (carpet), Johns Manville (insulation) and MiTek (building products, primarily connector plates used in roofing) are all materially affected by construction activity."

In aggregate, the five housing-related companies had pretax profits of $513 million in 2011. That's similar to 2010, but down from $1.8 billion in 2006.

> *"Housing will come back—you can be sure of that. Over time, the number of housing units necessarily matches the number of households (after allowing for a normal level of vacancies). For a period of years prior to 2008, however, America added more housing units than households. Inevitably, we ended up with far too many units and the bubble popped with a violence that shook the entire economy. That created still another unexpected problem for housing: Early in a recession, household formations slow, and in 2009 the decrease was dramatic."*

Warren also noted, "At [the nation's current] annual pace of 600,000 housing starts—considerably less than the number of new households being formed—buyers and renters are sopping up what's left of the old oversupply. (This process will run its course at different rates around the country; the supply-demand situation varies widely by locale.) While this healing takes place, however, Berkshire's housing-related companies sputter, employing only 43,315 people compared to 58,769 in 2006."

However, Warren was still bullish. The Berkshire mantra of buy and hold remained in place ("Our favorite holding period is forever"), despite the hit that the construction field had taken. He summed up his feelings in his letter to shareholders as follows:

> *This hugely important sector of the economy, which includes not only construction but everything that feeds off of it, remains in a depression of its own. I believe this is the major reason a recovery in employment has so severely lagged the steady and substantial comeback we have seen in almost all other sectors of our economy.*
>
> *Wise monetary and fiscal policies play an important role in tempering recessions, but these tools don't create*

households nor eliminate excess housing units. Fortunately, demographics and our market system will restore the needed balance—probably before long. When that day comes, we will again build one million or more residential units annually. I believe pundits will be surprised at how far unemployment drops once that happens. They will then reawake to what has been true since 1776: America's best days lie ahead.

The housing bubble was unexpected, but Warren said that you can still expect couples to want to form families. "That devastating supply/demand equation is now reversed: Every day we are creating more households than housing units. People may postpone hitching up during uncertain times, but eventually hormones take over. And while 'doubling-up' may be the initial reaction of some during a recession, living with in-laws can quickly lose its allure."

10 Ways in Which Deals Can Unexpectedly Turn Ugly

When you are looking at the deal, don't just look at the pretty parts. You should be looking at the whole thing.

A broken play is exactly what it sounds like: a meeting that, for one reason or another, doesn't go the way you want it to go. And there are a lot of things that can alter your hopes for how a meeting plays out. Here are 10 examples of the unexpected that can put a dent in your deal making:

1. *People.* The wrong people from the prospect company come to the meeting. Some of your people can't attend the meeting at the last minute.

2. *Technology.* The Internet connection, your technology demonstration,

=== WARREN WAY 88 ===

Do Your Homework

"Risk is not knowing what you are doing," says Warren.

the projector, the phone for a conference call—whatever it is you need—doesn't work.

3. *Facility.* The room holds 8 people, and 12 were invited. The room holds 250 people, and 12 were invited. The room is too hot or too cold. The room location has changed, and half the attendees don't know the new location.

4. *Hostility.* Someone has a personal agenda to damage this relationship, and this person asks distracting questions, points out tiny details, and dominates the meeting—all to cast you in an unfavorable light.

5. *Time.* The time of the meeting gets moved at the last minute. An hour meeting becomes a half-hour meeting without notice.

6. *Disruption.* People arrive late or leave early. Someone interrupts to take a vote on the lunch menu. Two people whisper together throughout the meeting. The fire alarm rings and you have to leave the building for 15 minutes. A sudden summer thunderstorm forces people to leave the meeting to roll up car windows.

7. *Distraction.* Jackhammers break up the sidewalk outside the window. The next-door office has a raucous retirement party. Seminar-goers from down the hall stop outside your door to visit during a restroom break.

8. *Tangent.* Someone makes a comment, and the entire conversation shifts to a totally new topic and never returns to the subject at hand.

9. *Usurper.* Someone feels the need to be important and peppers your presentation with asides—sometimes funny ones—that keep you off track.

10. *Preparation.* Attendees are not prepared, so you waste valuable time having to establish a background that they should already know.

When any of these events, or other ones, threatens to disrupt the purpose of your meeting, declare it a broken play:

> *"I'm sorry, but we all agreed upon some outcomes for today's meeting, and, based on the circumstances, I think it will be difficult to get them. Let's reset our outcomes so that they reflect what we think we can achieve and meet again. We want to make our time spent together valuable."*

Never Trust Your Technology Demo

Be prepared to pitch with a smooth transition if your demo blows up. I have seen techno-demos become techno-dramas several times. It may be an important part of your pitch. It might even be the whole reason for the meeting, but if it blows up, you have to be prepared to address it and move on. Steve Swanson of Imperial CRS says: "Rarely is there not a broken play, usually around technology. But we've found if we can name it, that made it better. Declaring the broken play, our customers have been so genuine that they've gone overboard in trying to make it up to us."

How to Prepare for Unpredictable Problems

Don't ever accept the idea of, "Well, let's just see how far we can get." This is a weak answer, and it doesn't show respect for you or for your efforts. Worse, a well-developed presentation requires all the materials that were designed, not just a sound bite or an ESPN Sports Center highlight reel. You have to make certain that you have come to a specific definition of outcomes that everyone believes are possible, or you have to cancel the meeting and reschedule.

Enrich your deal-making practice sessions further by adding one or more broken plays to the meetings you're practicing. Adding a broken-play element changes your presentation entirely. To make it even more realistic, don't tell your team members what the broken play is until they begin their rehearsal. Most often, broken plays happen without notice during a meeting, so practice that way.

Before you prepare to go, you should always confirm the date, time, place, size of room, and *confirmed attendees* the morning of the meeting. There is too much on the line just to assume that all these details will take care of themselves.

Another thing you can do to ensure that the meeting goes as well as possible is to warm up the room when you open the meeting. The key here is to get prospects talking from the opening—loosening up and engaging. Giving a pitch for 30 to 45 minutes and then asking, "Are there any questions?" doesn't give you the kind of interaction you need for a win. If you want your pitch to be successful, I encourage you to open the meeting with a question that will get your prospects to talk for 10 minutes. Two of our favorites are:

1. "What has changed in your business/department since the last time we spoke?"
2. "What's the most important thing each of you wants to get out of today's meeting?"

These questions will let you have more control over the meetings and keep you on track to achieve the outcomes you want. Your goal is to minimize the unexpected.

Profile Your Prospects

Become a student of human psychology. Try to analyze those around you. This will help you draw up profiles of the members of your prospect's team. Begin with individual profiles.

1. Determine each person's fears.

2. Identify disruptions in people's personal lives that might cause lack of attention or interest, such as ill children, divorce proceedings, or recent deaths in families.
3. Determine each person's viewpoint on your solution.
4. Note any other personality traits, events, or characteristics that might affect individuals.

Then profile the team.

1. Be aware of the team dynamics.
2. Determine whether the team's fears are different from individuals' fears.
3. Watch where people sit at the table.
4. Notice whether team members defer to certain people and cut off certain others.

Begin these profiles the first time you meet anyone in the prospect company. Add to them. Keep them updated. Use them to your advantage.

Here are some of the types of people you're likely to meet at your prospect's table during your next big Warren Buffett deal. Keep these four kinds of people in mind.

Most Dangerous: The Eel

The most dangerous of all the people who will be involved in this deal is the one we call the eel. In every deal, and at every prospect's table, there is always an eel—a person who is against the deal. *Always.*

WARREN WAY 68

Judging Humans Is Imperfect at Best
"There is no way to eliminate the possibility
of error when judging humans."

Eels have a tendency to hang out in the shadows. They're hard to get to, and they usually talk you down when you're not around. The conversation may be innocuous and sound like one of these three statements:

1. "I'm just concerned that we might be taking on too much right now with a change."
2. "Let's bring this deal in after the SAP upgrade gets completed."
3. "Don't get me wrong, I think this is a great idea. I just wish we had the resources to support it."

Most likely, these people are fearful and don't want to acknowledge it; instead, they'll say that they're against the deal on principle. Maybe they're afraid they'll be made to look bad if a new vendor is brought on. Or maybe they're just curmudgeons who don't want to see change.

Whatever the reason, be afraid. Be very afraid. Eels have the power to kill you. You have to identify your eels early in the process and decide how to handle them. Here are our suggestions:

1. *Co-opt them.* Take the eel's ideas and bake them into your solution. Give credit liberally and frequently to your eel.

2. *Pair them up.* Find someone in your organization who speaks the eel's language. Maybe they match each other in education, age, or style. Whatever it is, this will create a friendly link for back-channel dialogue that will turn the eel or, at the very least, neutralize his negativity.

3. *Containment.* This is a combination of conceding all this person's small issues and points, then turning the conversation to the resolution of the bigger issues. You have to limit the person's scope of influence on your deal to items that are contained rather than allowing her issues to fester into deal killers.

4. *Find them another bone.* Sometimes a curmudgeon wears out his welcome and his interest in a deal. Your job is to have enough knowledge of the company and its issues to refocus the eel on another part of the world that is not your deal.

Most Annoying: The Expert

The person from the prospect company who may most test your patience is the so-called expert, otherwise known as "the idiot who thinks he knows everything, and for some reason, everyone in the prospect company listens to him."

When you bring your new and complicated solution to your prospect, the rest of the firm turns to the only light of information people have and trust... one of their own. As the "smartest person," the expert knows everything about the topic in question. Experts are trusted implicitly and completely, even when they're totally wrong.

Because of this trust on the part of their colleagues, experts have to be treated differently from anyone else. Here are some suggestions on how to deal with the expert:

1. *Eliminate from consideration.* This almost never works unless your champion has always suspected that the expert was not that knowledgeable. Be very careful. An expert enjoys protected class status, and the attempt to eliminate her by showing her up can have consequences. The expert is on site or in the firm, and she has both professional and personal relationships with others in the firm. The "nobody picks on my sister but me" mentality can take over, and you will be shut out.

2. *Ignore.* Sometimes ignoring the expert is the wisest thing you can do. Until you know the lay of the land, simply treat the expert as another person at the prospect's table. His questions and comments have merit and weight equal to everyone else's, *but no more* than anyone else's. This play works well if you can keep the expert looking informed, but not smart. It's advantageous to agree that the expert from the prospect's team is knowledgeable, but the expertise exists in your team.

3. *Marginalize.* This involves creating clear boundaries for where the expert's knowledge ends. In this way, experts can feel validated about their knowledge and can even receive compliments from you, while, at the same time, their potential impact on the overall process can be minimized.

4. *Engage*. This solution is fraught with peril. To engage the expert is to let her opinion dominate the dialogue. Unless the expert is your firm advocate *and* clearly has the ear of the ultimate prospect, she can become dictatorial as a result of your endorsement of her knowledge. If you choose to engage experts, you must educate them from their current point of information until they actually do achieve expert status. In this way, you solidify their power base and at the same time make yourself indispensable to their future roles.

5. *Convert*. This strategy is for the expert who has clearly chosen a different solution or who has "seen it all" and just knows that your solution is not going to be effective. Instead of coercion or conversion, it is best to attempt collaboration. In this scenario, bring the expert closer and ask lots of questions. Provide no statements or rebuttals until all the thoughts are out on the table. Use questions to encourage the expert to move to your way of thinking.

Experts often rely on their role as expert. They are not easily replaced or eliminated, and although their true knowledge of the subject matter may be limited, their knowledge of the organization is greater than yours. Craft a strategy that puts the expert inside your circle and managing the decision-making process with you, instead of outside your circle directing the process toward you.

Most Frustrating: The In Crowd

Here are descriptions of three additional types who will show up, sooner or later, at your prospect's table.

1. *Indifferent*. In any large, complex sale, indifference—or a show of indifference—may be a characteristic that you face quite often. Large sales take a great deal of time and include many people. In the beginning of the process, some people may be asked to partici-pate who really don't have a dog in the fight. With any luck, they either will self-select out of future meetings or will be asked to stop coming.

However, if one person is indifferent in the beginning and continues to be part of your discussions, you need to find a way to get rid of him. Indifference is like a giant black storm cloud. If it's not addressed directly, it will encompass all your prospects and will either slow down or stop your deal.

Sometime prospects feign indifference in order to trick you into revealing more than you should. We all have a tendency to fill awkward silences with words, and indifferent people are experts at giving you awkward silences. One "Well, I just don't see what difference this will make," and many salespeople will be off and running, explaining and overexplaining to the point of providing free consulting.

Resist the urge to play this game. Either ask for more specifics or arrange a time to talk with the prospect in private. Negative, nonspecific complaints can give your entire discussion an air of uncertainty that you don't want and that certainly won't help your deal.

2. *Involved*. In a big hunt, the involved prospect can be one of your greatest blessings or one of your biggest nightmares. Involvement can speed your deal along. But it can also bog everything down and drive everyone—you, your team, and the other prospects—around the bend.

Your job is to amplify the blessing part and negate the nightmare part.

One of the best approaches to engaging an involved person productively is to meet in private before each meeting. Outline what you want to cover, and gather ideas for doing that in the best way. Emphasize the importance of reaching the outcomes you and the prospect have defined together. Reinforce with the involved person the need to avoid discussion of minor details that may be fascinating to one individual, but that are of no interest to the other people on the prospect's team.

If you make involved people part of your solution—that is, if you engage them fully in the sales process you have outlined—they can be extremely valuable in helping you move from step to step.

But if you leave them alone, they will slow down your meetings and your overall movement toward closing.

3. *In denial*. The in-denial prospect doesn't see any reason for going through this exercise. Such a person views change as an enemy and prefers that the company continue doing things the way "we've always done them here."

From the beginning of your dealings, this prospect will resist all your efforts. Because none of the people on your prospect's team are stupid, this one knows that your change will take place. But in no way will she make it easy for you. You may be asked the same questions repeatedly while the prospect burrows into your solution and picks out various small items to argue with you about. This kind of behavior can throw meetings off track by beginning a tangential discussion.

People who are in denial may be vocally supportive of whatever you suggest. But if they are given a task, they'll never complete it, for one reason or another. Because they are vocally supportive, it's very hard to spot and label in-denial prospects. But remember that actions speak louder than words.

Your best bet here is to get rid of this person, if at all possible. If you don't, the toxicity will wear out you and your team.

If you can't get rid of the people and you have to deal with them, then you must take the following three steps. Step one, raise awareness of the data and information that is in conflict with their current form of reference. Step two, provide context why the outside information is really valid to their situation. And, step three, forecast the impact of what will happen if you stay on the current path. The only way people will make new decisions is when they get new information that they determine is relevant.

Most Obnoxious: Plain Old Liars

Let's look at the liars, fibbers, half-truth-tellers, "concealers," and delusional hopefuls, whose greatest sin is that they lie to themselves first and then repeat it to us.

We don't have science behind us, and we are wary of the pop-psychological world of body language interpretation: "If he looks down and to the left, he's lying." We do, however, tend to think that there are some indicators that the conversation is not completely truthful, and that those hints are worth watching for.

1. *Excessive claims.* The promises that a person is making are too big for the person's position in the company or role in the project. We saw this recently with an information technology manager at a client's prospect who wanted to buy the solution badly, but who was in no position to make the buy. He was making the claim that he could approve the deal because he was zealous, and also because he was afraid we'd move past him and leave him out of the discussions.

2. *Wait and see.* When someone is delaying the timeline in a buying process that she defined, it's not a great indicator of honesty. We have found that in these circumstances, the person is often checking pricing with the incumbent vendor or negotiating with your biggest competitor while keeping you on the hook.

3. *Too good to be true.* "Price is not a major factor in this decision." "We're not considering any other providers." "We're going to bypass the normal testing phases and put this into full production." We've heard all of these, and later in the process, not one of them turned out to be true. Was the person lying? Let's say no. But we think he had convinced himself of something that he should have known was not going to be true in the end.

4. *If, then.* For example, you are told, "If you just lower your price 11 percent, then we will make the decision right away," only to find out that this was a gambit in a list of demands. This liar is seductive because she preys upon our sense of urgency and causes us to act as her agent in negotiations within our own firm. The "if, then" liars proceed to blame other forces within their firm for further delays and heretofore unmentioned requirements as a means of repeating the "if, then" game to win even more concessions.

When we see these types of red flags, we push. We think a mixture of self-confidence, raw curiosity, and authenticity can get you closer to the truth, regardless of whether the person will tell you the truth or not. The biggest push is raw curiosity—asking is raw curiosity—so ask the questions that are uncomfortable. It always surprises us how often we don't ask the questions we know we should because we are afraid of the answer—as if by not asking the question, we can make the answer not exist.

Some of those tough questions can include

1. Why are you considering making a change at this time?
2. What is the exact threshold of performance improvement that has to be achieved for us to win this business?
3. Who has the greatest amount to lose in your company if you agree to do business with us?
4. Since you are delaying the decision for 30 days, what specifically will change during that period to enable you to make a better decision in 30 days?
5. If you made the decision today and went with our firm, what is the biggest thing that could go wrong? Who would be the first to point it out?

Here is a suggestion: using the profiles you have of your prospects, practice one or more meetings that will be part of your process.

1. Designate two or three team members to play the parts of your prospects, coming as close as possible to the behavior that each person would exhibit.
2. Have two or three of your team members play themselves.
3. Give your presentation.

You'll be surprised at how difficult this can be. Until you've practiced over and over, it's hard to be assured and natural when issues arise. If your team members can get into the minds of your prospects, you'll be amazed at what they will come up with.

Switch players and roles until you and your team are ready for any possible occurrence. When you expect the unexpected, you can be ready for anything.

Buffett Bonus | Be Candid About What You Expect in a Deal

When Buffett is out to make a deal, he knows exactly what he wants. He also tends to make deals in clusters: insurance companies, furniture retailers, construction products, candies and confections, shoes and footwear, jewelry, and so on. He wants businesses that he understands and whose products he expects people to want in the future. Of course, he also likes a consistent earnings history and a good return on equity with little debt. Perhaps most important of all, he likes honest and hardworking managers. When the economics are right and the company has trustworthy people in charge, you can expect that he will make a deal. These are not secrets we have uncovered. He talks about these in his writings, his interviews, and his public speaking.

LESSON 14

Don't Fight,
But When You Do...

Warren is a lover, not a fighter. He loves his work, and he chooses to make deals with people he loves to work with. However, there are exceptions.

Naturally, not all of Warren's deals have gone smoothly (nobody is perfect). Back in 1987, Berkshire purchased a 12 percent stake in Salomon Brothers, making it the largest shareholder and Warren a director of the investment banking firm. In 1990, a scandal involving John Gutfreund, the CEO of Salomon Brothers at the time, surfaced.

"Buffett always did fall in love with people, and observers said he was noticeably in love with Gutfreund—at first," wrote Warren's biographer, Alice Schroeder.[9]

While the dealings at Salomon have filled many books, here was the issue in a nutshell: a rogue trader at Salomon was submitting bids in excess of what was allowed by U.S. Treasury rules. When Gutfreund learned about it, he failed to suspend the individual immediately. Gutfreund left the company in August 1991, and Warren became chairman until the crisis passed.

In September 1991, Warren was called to testify before Congress. His testimony was chilling. "I want to find out exactly what happened in the past so that the stain is borne by the guilty few," he said, "and removed from the innocent."

What Warren stood for in deal making was on display for the entire world to see. He asked the government to aid in the crackdown and employ the full judicial powers at its disposal. "Lose money for the firm, and I will be understanding," testified Warren. "Lose a shred of reputation for the firm, and I will be ruthless."

Make Deals, Not War

Let's say you're making a deal, a complex and sizable deal, and one of the members of the prospect's team starts going south on you. We don't mean disagreeing with you or questioning you; we mean active hostility. He won't return your phone calls or e-mails, misses commitments, pushes back on requests, and challenges your capabilities, truthfulness, and lineage. You get the picture.

You know that this person is critical to the deal, but he is not the decision maker—he's more like a piece of the machinery. You have to get the prospect's executive leadership to bring him to heel. Let's assume that you've tried all the traditional get-along strategies: collaboration, cooperation, compromise, flattery, and bribery.

It's time to fight. And sometimes you have to fight. Let's talk about a few rules:

Rule 1: *You do not talk about Fight Club.* If you're making the move to fight, don't talk about it, either internally or externally. If your prospect, your people, or anyone else asks you, the answer is: "We're just working through a few issues right now, but things are going well in general." At some point, you will have to play nice with whoever's left standing; don't gloat to your friends, and don't warn your enemies.

Rule 2: *Go all Sun-Tzu on them.* The ancient Chinese military strategist said, "The greatest generals win without battle." Weigh your options one more time. Can you win this deal without a fight? It's the better way to get what you want.

Rule 3: *Never fight down.* If you're going to fight out an issue, you go over the person's head. You have one shot at this, and you'll need the most senior person at the prospect's table to bring authority to bear.

Rule 4: *Just the facts.* Your opinions, the other person's intentions, the he-said/she-said of conversations—they all make you look weak. Besides that, your opponent will go back to your supporters at the company after the phone call or meeting and retell the story, spinning it in her favor. Stick to the facts, the documents, the numbers, timelines, e-mails, meeting notes... you get it.

Rule 5: *Ask questions; make few statements.* Is this how your company normally handles these types of requests? Is this what working together will be like once we close this deal? What parts of your process, as we have discussed it, are we not understanding or fulfilling our part of? You want to ask questions, but just like a good attorney, you have to know the answers before you ask the questions.

Rule 6: *Concede the little points.* There has to be some ground you can give. Everyone believes there are two sides to the story, so be ready to give on some issues that are not material but that show balance. Stay focused on the core issues of the fight.

Rule 7: *Win, don't wound.* If you have to fight, play for keeps. You never back a snake into a corner and then turn to walk away. No jabs—just throw the haymakers, get the issue on the table, and then resolve it. Make it clean and fast, and move on.

WARREN WAY 55

Pick Your Battles

Buffett learned this during his dealings with Salomon. "I could have fought harder and been more vocal. I might have felt better about myself if I did. But it wouldn't have changed the course of history. Unless you sort of enjoy combat, it doesn't make sense."

Rule 8: *Leave an exit.* You have to leave a way out for your opponent after you've won the fight. Look, big companies won't fire your opponents. They'll keep them. So you have to have a way to let those people save face. Easy ones to use are change of scope, confusion, misunderstanding, and the like. The point is, once you've won the fight, it is absolutely imperative that you be gracious. Remember, you may very well have to deal with this person for a long time.

Let us be very clear. When it's come to fights in the past, we've lost more than we've won for one simple reason: our opponent has been on the inside, while we were on the outside. The insider has the high ground in combat, so you have to exhaust every other angle first. This is a last-ditch effort. Sometimes it works, and that's good enough for the effort, but often all you get out of it is the moral righteousness of having left without regrets. There isn't much money in moral righteousness these days.

Buffett Bonus | No Bluffing. No Kidding

"We don't bluff. It's not my style anyway," says Buffett. "Over a lifetime, you'll get a reputation for bluffing or not bluffing. And therefore, I want it to be understood that I don't do it." This goes for his deal making and his commitment to integrity. At Salomon, he put out a one-page letter to employees that insisted that they report all legal violations and unethical behavior to him. He included his home phone number on the letter. He wanted Salomon to pass what he called "the front-page test." The letter said: "I want employees to ask themselves whether they are willing to have any contemplated act appear the next day on the front page of their local paper, to be read by their spouses, children, and friends, with the reporting done by an informed and critical reporter."

If You Want to Marry, Don't Tarry

WARREN HAS a penchant for fast deals.

When he bought 90 percent of the gargantuan Nebraska Furniture Mart from Rose Blumkin—the famous Mrs. B—for $55 million in one day, Warren learned a valuable lesson. He explained his mistake six years later in his 1988 letter to Berkshire shareholders.

"Your Chairman blundered then by neglecting to ask Mrs. B a question any schoolboy would have thought of: 'Are there any more at home like you?' Last month I corrected the error: We are now 80 percent partners with another branch of the family."

When the opportunity presented itself, Warren did not hesitate to obtain the stake in Borsheims, the 25,400-square-foot Omaha jewelry and tabletop furnishings store run by the other half of the family, the Friedmans.

"Most people, no matter how sophisticated they are in other matters, feel like babes in the woods when purchasing jewelry," wrote Warren in his 1988 letter to Berkshire stockholders. "They can judge neither quality nor price. For them only one rule makes sense: If you don't know jewelry, know the jeweler."

Blumkin escaped from Russia after the revolution in 1917 to join two siblings in America, and her parents and her other five siblings followed. Among the sisters was Rebecca Friedman, who, with her husband, Louis, escaped to the West in 1922. When the family members reunited in Omaha, they had no tangible assets, but they managed to achieve remarkable rags-to-riches success in retailing.

In 1948, the Friedmans purchased Borsheims, a small Omaha jewelry store. They were joined in the business by their son, Ike, in 1950 and, as the years went by, by Ike's son, Alan; their sons-in-law, Marvin Cohn and Donald Yale, came in also.

Warren explained the courtship as follows: "I can assure you that those who put their trust in Ike Friedman and his family will never be disappointed. The way in which we purchased our interest in their business is the ultimate testimonial. Borsheims had no audited financial statements; nevertheless, we didn't take inventory, verify receivables or audit the operation in any way. Ike simply told us what was so—and on that basis we drew up a one-page contract and wrote a large check."

Business at Borsheims has mushroomed in recent years as the reputation of the Friedman family has spread. Customers now come to the store from all over the country. Among them have been some friends of mine from both coasts who thanked me later for getting them there.

Borsheims was in Warren's backyard. "It is great fun to be in business with people you have long admired," said Warren. "The Friedmans, like the Blumkins, have achieved success because they have deserved success. Both families focus on what's right for the customer and that, inevitably, works out well for them, also. We couldn't have better partners."

The Borsheims store in Omaha now covers more than 62,500 square feet after its 2006 remodeling, and it maintains an inventory that includes more than 100,000 pieces.

In 2012, for the second consecutive year, Warren set sales records selling jewelry during the May shareholders' weekend, which attracts more than 35,000 Berkshire Hathaway shareholders, members of the media, and other guests to Omaha. In fact, Adrienne Fay, director of marketing and advertising at Borsheims, says that the shareholders' weekend outperforms the holiday season.

Warren admits that he is a shameless promoter. "I will be clerking at Borsheims, desperate to beat my sales figure from last year," Buffett wrote in the 2012 letter to stockholders. "So come take advantage of me. Ask me for my 'Crazy Warren' price."

Don't Delay, Because Time Kills Deals

For most of the big deals that we have been a part of closing or have heard about, the closing was not an event that happened in a room with a contract and a big fat pen.

The same will probably be true of your next big Warren Buffett–style deal. The real close and the real decision to do the deal will probably happen when you aren't around. Possibly, you won't even know the location or the exact time. What will really happen and what will really be said—at the moment in which people will look across the table at one another and agree to proceed—is not usually recorded, at least not in detail.

=== WARREN WAY 44 ===

Seek Simplicity in Deals

Don't overcomplicate agreements. "The business schools reward difficult complex behavior more than simple behavior, but simple behavior is most effective."

The closing of your next big deal, like that of all other deals, will be messy. It'll be disorganized. And perhaps it'll be a bit capricious. All of which means that people will be involved.

Communication happens in both organized and disorganized fashions, including the following:

1. *Formal review* of your solution in a boardroom setting with a decision-making team.

2. *Water cooler lobbying* with the whispered, "What did you think of that proposal from XYZ?"

3. *Survivor*-style antics, including alliances, surprises, and power plays.

4. *Reference checking* or other social proof that is needed before pulling the trigger.

5. *Key decision maker contacting you* for predecision negotiations. (These approaches sound like this: "If you guys get this deal, would you be able to start in two weeks instead of six weeks?" or some other change in the original scope.)

6. *Advocate steering.* Your advocate contacts you for some coaching on things to do, points you are losing that you can still win, and how to do it.

7. *Internal sabotage.* People who feel that they are at risk use all means available to derail the deal so that the work stays in their area, department, and budget.

The list can go on and on. The point is this: closing is not a definable moment in time.

Let's Not Kid Ourselves

The idea that the "close" of a big deal is something for which I can give you a trick or a technique to secure a seven-, eight-, or nine-figure deal is intellectually dishonest.

Think of closing your Warren Buffett kind of deal as being a lot like watching legislation get passed. There's what goes on in front of the cameras, and there's what happens behind closed doors.

In front of the cameras, the legislative process is governed by an arcane set of guidelines called Robert's Rules of Order. Behind the closed doors, it's the Wild, Wild West.

In front of the cameras, your next big deal hunt will typically have an orchestrated and somewhat professional process described to you by the prospect company. It's an ideal that represents how the mythical "average" deal is decided. Following are the steps in that process.

Step 1. Collection of information

Step 2. Review

Step 3. Final consideration

Step 4. The award

Step 5. The save

What we'll do now is break down the closing process into the steps listed here and discuss some ideas on how to win in "the process behind the closed doors."

Collecting Closing Info

You may be thinking, "Wait a minute—we've met, we've talked, and I've submitted my solution. Isn't that the end of the collection of information?" Not really. Your prospect or prospects are still getting all the data they can on you and your solution. This means asking clarifying questions about your solution, making secondary requests for corroborating information, addendum inquiries, and so on.

As you receive these questions, you want to be helpful, thorough, and responsive. You also want to use this as a reconnaissance period for your own gathering of information.

━━━━━━━━━━ WARREN WAY 38 ━━━━━━━━━━

Don't Adopt Sloppy Deal-Making Habits

"Chains of habit are too light to be felt until
they are too heavy to be broken."

Simple Rule: If You Are Asked a Question, Ask a Question Yourself

After you have given a thorough answer to the questions that have been asked of you, extend the discussion to include the following kinds of questions of your own:

"What is important to you about this area of the solution?"
"What's the biggest area of confusion for the prospects around this?"
"Is there additional material I can provide that would be helpful in this area?"

This is a period during which your best approach is to be responsive and thorough. Your prospects are driving this part of the process. However, if you have a strong champion, you want to ask her the following questions during this phase:

1. What are the people hung up on?
2. Is any one of the solutions standing out in the process so far?
3. Are there any red flags? What are they?

During this phase, you are looking for the bookends of the discussion:

1. What is out in front in terms of approaches, pricing, or solution detail?
2. What is the major concern of those who have taken a first reading of the solutions?

There is plenty of runway left in the closing process, so gather this information while you still have enough time to react to either cement your lead or correct your shortcomings.

Buffett Bonus | Sometimes You Can't Hurry Love or Deals

The idea that you can't force deals does not contradict the value of speed. Delay kills deals, so proceed with all due haste. But don't make mistakes because you went too fast. Buffett says: "In the search, we adopt the same attitude one might find appropriate in looking for a spouse: It pays to be active, interested, and open-minded, but it does not pay to be in a hurry."

How do you know if the deal is the right one? Buffett told the *Wall Street Journal*: "It's like when you marry a girl. Is it her eyes? Her personality? It's a whole bunch of things you can't separate." However, when you decide that this is the one to go for, then go out and make it happen.

The Final Hour

WARREN ALMOST lost his sweetest deal in the final hour. He was willing to pay three times book for a California maker of boxed chocolates, but it wasn't enough.

"When you hit your choking point, you quit," says Buffett. "I've walked away from deals before and meant it. I walked away from the See's deal. They wanted $30 million, and we offered $25 million. We walked away and, fortunately for us, they walked after us," he said.

Warren did not fully come into his own as a dealmaker until he and his partner, Charles Munger, collaborated on the deal to acquire See's Candies in 1972. Before that, Warren had never paid more for a company than its book value.[10]

For those who have never seen or tasted this California confection, the image of the grandmotherly, bespectacled, silver-haired Mary See still smiles with pride from candy boxes shipped throughout the world. Back in 1921, Charles See chose the image of his mother when he arrived in Los Angeles from Canada to try his hand at the confection business. Charles, along with his mother and his wife, Florence, opened the first See's Candies shop and kitchen in Los Angeles.

The sparkling clean, black-and-white shop was designed to resemble Mary See's home kitchen. The high-quality candy was a hit, and See's had grown to 12 shops by the mid-1920s and 30 shops during the Depression. By 1936, See's was able to expand to San Francisco.

Mary See died in 1939 at the age of 85, but the company was able to adjust.

Following World War II, California's population surged, and the family opened shops throughout the state. In the 1950s, See's embraced the new and growing phenomenon of shopping malls and located stores there. Whatever the location, See's retained the old-fashioned black-and-white décor.

Today, See's candies are sold in more than 200 shops throughout the West and at many airport kiosks. The company's revenues are highly seasonal, with about half of the total annual revenues being earned in the months of November and December.

"At See's, annual sales were 16 million pounds of candy when Blue Chip Stamps purchased the company in 1972," Warren wrote in his 2007 annual letter to shareholders. "(Charlie and I controlled Blue Chip at the time and later merged it into Berkshire.) Last year See's sold 31 million pounds, a growth rate of only 2% annually. Yet its durable competitive advantage, built by the See's family over a 50-year period, and strengthened subsequently by Chuck Huggins and Brad Kinstler, has produced extraordinary results for Berkshire."

Warren will not invest in a business unless he feels reasonably certain of how much it will earn over the next 20 to 25 years. But for all of Warren's deal-making savvy, he does not feel truly comfortable unless a business has a brand-name product that would appeal to him.

"Long-term competitive advantage in a stable industry is what we seek in a business," wrote Warren in 2007. "If that comes with rapid organic growth, great. But even without organic growth, such a business is rewarding."

Here is how Warren described the money end of the deal in his 2007 letter to shareholders.

Let's look at the prototype of a dream business, our own See's Candy. The boxed-chocolates industry in which it operates is unexciting: Per-capita consumption in the U.S. is extremely low and doesn't grow. Many once-important brands have disappeared, and only three companies have earned more than token profits over the last forty years. Indeed, I believe that See's, though it obtains the bulk of its revenues from only a few states, accounts for nearly half of the entire industry's earnings....

We bought See's for $25 million when its sales were $30 million and pre-tax earnings were less than $5 million. The capital then required to conduct the business was $8 million. (Modest seasonal debt was also needed for a few months each year.) Consequently, the company was earning 60% pre-tax on invested capital. Two factors helped to minimize the funds required for operations. First, the product was sold for cash, and that eliminated accounts receivable. Second, the production and distribution cycle was short, which minimized inventories.

In 2007, Warren reported that See's sales were $383 million, and pretax profits were $82 million. The capital then required to run the business was $40 million. Warren knew there aren't many businesses like See's in corporate America. He explained to shareholders that companies that increase their earnings from $5 million to $82 million generally require approximately 10 times the capital investment that See's did to finance their growth.

A postscript to the See's math: after paying corporate taxes on the profits, Berkshire used the rest to make deals for other attractive businesses. As Warren said in his 2007 letter, "Just as Adam and Eve kick-started an activity that led to six billion humans, See's has given birth to multiple new streams of cash for us. (The biblical command to 'be fruitful and multiply' is one we take seriously at Berkshire.)"

Warren considers See's one of his biggest failures, not one of his biggest success stories. Why? Because he almost let this deal get away.

Run the Race to the Finish

Don't fool yourself that review doesn't start until the official presentation or proposal has been received. Review starts way before that.

Allow us to illustrate what we mean.

One of the biggest deals that coauthor Tom ever landed was for an outsourced call center for an international logistics and shipping company. The review process was arduous. The process went on for four months, with site visits, interviews, presentations—the works. The company had considered ten semifinalist companies and was now reviewing the three finalists for a multiyear, multi-multimillion-dollar deal.

One of the three finalist companies sent in its final proposal response overnight, using the *prospect's competitor's* service. The prospect received the response and dropped it in the trash unopened. That was a little mistake with a big negative outcome. Obviously the company that sent in the proposal had told someone at its own front desk to send it out overnight. That person didn't know what was in the package and didn't consider what sending it in that envelope might mean.

When you are being reviewed and perhaps compared with other companies, remember that there is no universally held set of beliefs within your prospect's company about *how* it should select the right vendor.

Each member of the team (or, for that matter, a husband and wife deciding to buy life insurance) has his own set of consider-

---

==== WARREN WAY 96 ====

If You Smell a Bad Deal, Do What You Can to Get Out Gracefully

"Should you find yourself in a chronically leaking boat, energy devoted to changing vessels is likely to be more productive than energy devoted to patching leaks."

ations to bring to the table. Even in a completely unbiased discussion with no previous preferences for a provider (which *never* happens), people are bringing a predisposition to favor one type of response or another.

You have to be prepared to do the following:

1. Present your solution for everyone who will read or hear it as if you were talking or writing for that person only.
2. Influence comparisons with other vendors if they are asked to be part of the process.
3. Shape the discussion.

These steps are what it'll take to set up the circumstances for your next big Warren Buffett kind of deal to be awarded to you. We know of only a few deals in which the winning person or company submitted the solution, then stood back and waited for the answer. The vast majority of deals that have been won, and almost all of our big deals, required vigilance through this stage in the process.

Let's say that your only voice during this stage of the closing process will be the documents you submit. Your solution, pricing sheets, addendums, and so on, will be the basis for the decision.

Even though you have submitted logical and well-thought-out materials, don't think for a minute that the process will be logical and well thought out. There are people involved! That means that this process can turn left or right on a whim.

If you start with the idea that you won't be in the room after your solution is presented, how do you present or write that solution?

We'll start with some ideas that you have probably already done, well before the closing stage. But just in case you haven't, you need to do them now.

Preliminary

1. Do Your Homework

We don't like games of chance when it comes to sales, and probably neither do you.

First, to reduce your risk of missing the mark, you need to find out everything you can about the people who are going to review your solution.

Second, you need to know whether your solution has been farmed out to other vendors, and, if so, who they are.

Third, you need to understand the process of considering your solution, including what parts of the solution have the greatest importance to each person and to the buying company overall.

Fourth, what purchase decisions has the company made in the last 6 to 12 months, and what drove the selections that were made?

By doing this homework, you should be able to map out a presentation that is general and yet specific to the needs of your prospects.

2. Ask the Tough Questions Up Front

Start with the end in mind and keep it on your mind. Once you qualified your opportunity, your goal became closing the prospect in a process that involved submitting a solution. You want to get as much information as you can possibly obtain. So ask the questions before you begin preparing your presentation or proposal.

These questions include, but are not limited to, the following:

- What process does your company follow when it is making bigger decisions like this one?
- In the past, what has derailed companies like mine when they have tried to do work with your company?
- Of all the things your company looks at when it is considering a vendor or partner like me, what are the top three that really make the final difference?
- What are the performance thresholds that my company has to reach in order for you to change what you are currently doing?
- If we were to work together, what people on your team would need to feel comfortable with the processes that we would follow and the results that we would produce?

These questions are designed to get you the type of information that will allow you to provide the right answers for the right people in the solution. They also should allow you to steer around some of the land mines that are unseen but definitely out there in the prospect company when it considers your solution.

Preparing the Presentation or Proposal

1. Say or Write Something for Everybody

The finance people want to know the numbers. The operations people want to understand the process. The champion wants to see the core benefits in terms of time, money, and risk. Everyone who reads your solution is looking for something aimed at her. Not only does she want to see that it's in your solution, but she also wants to see it *the way she wants to see it*. This last piece is really important. It's not enough that this particular material is in your solution. You are responsible for making it *pop off the page* for the person who is looking for it.

We worked with a company that was pitching a very technical and complex solution to land its biggest deal ever. As we prepared the solution, the pricing and cost-justification documents went on for pages and pages. All of this material was necessary, but we knew that the real value was buried in the calculations and assumptions.

The CEO, COO, and CFO all needed to understand these numbers in detail. So, we created a three-part answer to this part of the solution. The first answer we titled at the top in bold letters, "The Bottom Line." It was just one page that showed the net business case impact for the first year and over three years. This was for the CEO.

The second part of the answer was titled at the top in bold letters, "How the Money Works." It was a several-page narrative about how we had created the business case and why it would work for the business. This was for the COO.

The last part of the answer was titled at the top, "The Business Case for Our Solution." This part was for the CFO, and it had all the materials from our original answer documents.

Not surprisingly, we received calls from each of the three. Each call included a "thank you," a few questions, and a comment at the end, "This helps a lot." When the deal was awarded and the two companies started working together, the statement that was made repeatedly was, "You guys just seemed to understand our business better."

The fact is, understanding the reader or prospect is understanding the business.

2. Focus on the How as Well as the What

We have written repeatedly that your company's competitive advantage is what gets you to the finalist list, but your ability to make your prospect feel comfortable and unafraid about buying from you is what lands you the deal. The way you accomplish this is through transparency—clearly showing how you will provide the benefits you offer, not just telling them what benefits you will achieve.

Every prospect is consciously or subconsciously hedging his bets. He is considering the question, "What if this doesn't work?" Should this happen, how will he deal with the results and handle the fallout? By showing the prospect your method for achieving the benefit, you are reassuring him the process is solid so that he will have greater confidence in the result.

Earlier in this book, we described one of our clients who landed a nine-figure deal that had been stalled for this very reason. The prospect wanted to work with the company but kept delaying the start. The cost-benefit was clear and significant. The credentials of the pitching company were solid. However, the delays were coming from the departments in the buying company because of fears of mistakes. Only when the company demonstrated all the processes and systems it would be using to deliver the program—the "how" of the benefits—was the deal closed and executed.

Using these ideas, you have presented or written a great solution that creates a strong case for you with the prospects when you are not there.

3. Bring In Your Closing Pitchers

This is one of the most effective techniques I have used and have had others use. Have the senior executives of one of your current satisfied clients call their counterparts in your prospect company during the period in which the review and comparison are being done. CEOs call CEOs, COOs call COOs, and so on. Ask them to leave a message on the person's voice mail that sounds something like this:

> *My name is _____. I am the (title) of ABC Company, a $100 million provider of (whatever it is ABC does). I understand that you are considering working with XYZ Company (your firm). I wanted to let you know that we have been working with them for X years, and they have been a great partner. One of the things they brought to the table that I appreciate is (insert a key issue benefit that you know is important to this prospect). I would be happy to talk with you about our experience with XYZ Company if you would like. You can reach me at your convenience at XXX-XXX-XXXX.*

It's great to have referrals and references early in the process, but just as baseball teams need a "closer" to finish out the game and hopefully secure a win, so do you.

4. Watch Out for a Huge Monkey Wrench to Be Thrown into the Works

Right before final consideration begins, the chances are good that someone on the prospect side will suggest that other vendors should be brought into the discussion. What do you do if your prospect's team members are enthusiastic about your solution but want to open the field for competition among you and your potential rivals?

Your first step is to find out what's behind this decision. You and your team have to do your due diligence to understand why your prospect is having this reaction. Is it something that you can affect? Or is it something that's beyond your control and influence? If this is the first you've heard of any of this, you have to take it as a red flag in terms of your potential relationship with the prospect, the support of your champion, the prospect's need for regulations, or perhaps your diligence in finding the right prospect in the first place.

Next, if you can stay and resolve the underlying issue that has led to this circumstance, that's certainly the best possible approach. Both you and your prospect will have learned how to work together to resolve mutual goals.

At this point, you may decide to walk away, and that's a legitimate decision. Just remember that you're leaving your solution behind you and handing over priceless free consulting. This will be a painful but useful lesson in selecting prospects and champions.

Or you might decide to stay and fight. If you choose to do this, though, you can't just lobby with a "we sure hope you buy from us" appeal. Your approach has to be more strategic than that.

Here are our suggestions on how to have a strategic and hopefully successful plan to stay and fight.

Suggestion 1

Throw the competition under the bus. In your marketplace, you and your competitors have quite a number of similarities. Admit it. Between you and your competitors, there are probably more aspects of your companies that are the same than that are different. Let's say there are 90 percent similarities and 10 percent differences.

The very best way to deal with the 90/10 situation is to acknowledge it and use it to your advantage. Point it out to the prospects. Make the list of what "everyone does" as long as you can.

Frame your discussion. Surely you have already defined the prospect's market conditions and then illustrated why you are and have the best solution.

You then explain why someone else's solution would be great *if your prospect or your competition were in different circumstances, which, of course, they aren't.*

One of the keys to this approach is to compliment your competitors. We know, we know, it seems counterintuitive.

But here's what you do.

Identify them as a good solution... in a very tiny set of conditions... none of which apply to your prospect or your competitors *at this time*. The language of these conversations follows this direction:

1. *Evolution*. Describe the industry, the market, and the customer base over a period of time and show what changes have taken place. In this model, you can talk about the world of the 1990s, the 2000s, and now. By describing the evolution, you can define competitors' advantages as addressing a world that no longer exists.

2. *Revolution*. Technology, regulation, offshore competitors, and other circumstances have revolutionized businesses. Placing your competitors as great prerevolution solutions is a good way to pigeonhole their value and emphasize yours.

3. *Devolution*. The world has gotten smaller—use language like "Competition locally required this... , competition nationally requires that... , and international competition demands something altogether different." Pigeonhole your competitors as great choices in a world in which competition is much more local.

Finally, of course, you have to point out that you are ready to meet your prospects' needs in the areas of money, time, and risk *right now*. Any other alternative would take much longer, cost more, and not be as well thought out as your solution is.

Suggestion 2

Recommend the questions that you want prospects to ask: "If it were me... ." These are the words that you want to plant in your prospect's ears. This has to be done carefully. You are not running down your competitors. Your role is to be an objective advisor to the prospects. You are advising them on what they should be looking at in the solutions. The "If it were me..." approach must be objective. This means that you have to be willing to withstand the scrutiny you are encouraging your prospects to give to all the solutions. Examples of this approach are:

If it were me, I would take a look at how each of the companies you are considering is sourcing its components. If they are
sourcing them offshore, you have to be concerned about quality
and safety stock.

If it were me, for each company submitting a solution, I would
want to see the financials for the last six months broken out
from the rest of the financial reports. There has been a lot of
volatility in my industry, and you want to make certain your
provider is strong enough.

If it were me, I would want a guarantee that the team each
competitor says is going to be dedicated to my account will be
the team that works it after the account is awarded. Our industry is famous for "bait and switch" on talent once an account is
awarded.

You can see that by taking this approach, you are arming the
prospect to push down on your competitors in ways that are *good
for the prospect.* It really is not about you, but it does put the prospect in a position to be informed and make a better selection. Our
assumption is that the better selection, because of the questions you
are teaching the prospect, will be you.

Suggestion 3

Probe for your own vulnerable spots. Assumptions are being made
and impressions formed about your company that you are not aware
of and possibly are not in control of. You have to figure out what
they are and how to influence them. One of the ways is to ask where
your solution is weak.

A client of ours almost lost a deal because his prospects were concerned that his financial support might not be strong enough if they
tripled their purchases from him over the next year. They didn't ask
him about his financial strength, however, nor did they indicate that
he might be receiving a 300 percent increase in orders from them in
the next year. Only because he asked each of the people at the prospect's table by phone, "In your mind, at this point, what would be the

number one thing that might keep us from working together?" did he find out the truth. He got on a plane with his CFO and his banker, visited the prospects, and closed the deal at that meeting.

In smaller deals, we are often very careful about bringing up the negatives. We have been taught that this is a bad thing. However, in your next big Warren Buffett kind of deal, what you do not know will kill you.

Buffett Bonus | Make Sure the Numbers Are Right

If you want to make deals like Buffett, the numbers represented by the other guy's money are critical to discussing the possibilities of working together. Too often, a deal-making discussion stops at budget. When you don't know about the other guy's money, ask—not for the trade secrets, but at least for the industry averages. If the prospect can't tell you, there are resources you can turn to in order to find out. This provides a basic financial framework for your discussion. This is obviously much easier to do for publicly traded companies that must publish annual reports with their financials. But Warren will often make a deal with a privately held company. For privately held companies, the numbers are fairly easy to estimate, at least the cost of goods sold, profit margin, and cash flow.

Here are Buffett's views from his 1996 annual report. "Your goal as an investor should be simply to purchase, at a rational price, a part interest in an easily understood business whose earnings are virtually certain to be materially higher, five, ten and twenty years from now. Over time, you will find only a few companies that meet those standards—so when you see one that qualifies, you should buy a meaningful amount of stock." Or, in Buffett's case, make a deal for the whole company.

The Last Step
Is Always Slippery

AFTER A brief deal-making hiatus, Berkshire Hathaway's March 14, 2011, decision to buy the Lubrizol Corporation for approximately $9 billion marked Warren's return to the mergers and acquisitions market. Lubrizol, based in Cleveland, is a chemical company that produces additives for gasoline, diesel fuel, engine oils, and other industrial lubricants.[11]

This was a nice addition for Warren, but apparently someone else had reasons to grease the deal.

David Sokol, a former star executive and potential candidate to replace Warren atop the Berkshire empire, faced a Securities and Exchange Commission inquiry shortly after the deal when it emerged that he had bought shares in Lubrizol while he was helping to make the deal to purchase the company. The case took center stage at Berkshire's annual meeting in 2011, after the Berkshire board accused Sokol of violating internal ethics and insider trading policies.

The Sokol affair was called a rare black eye for Warren. Sokol resigned weeks after the Lubrizol deal when it was revealed that he had bought about 100,000 Lubrizol shares (about a $10 million stake) shortly before bringing the company to Warren's attention.

Warren told the crowd of about 40,000 at the 2011 Berkshire annual meeting that he had made a "big mistake" in not quizzing the man who had once been regarded as his potential heir about the controversial share deal. The purchase netted Sokol about a $3 million profit. Not bad for a 90-day investment.

"I obviously made a big mistake by not saying, 'Well, when did you buy it?'" said Warren. He said he found Sokol's actions, taken by a man he had paid $24 million the previous year, to be "inexplicable" and "inexcusable." Media reports estimated Sokol's personal net worth at more than $100 million.

A regulatory filing detailing the Lubrizol purchase indicated that Sokol identified Lubrizol as a potential acquisition and took the lead in early negotiations to buy the company. Sokol had selected Lubrizol from a list of 18 chemical companies that bankers at Citigroup Global Markets had compiled in December 2010 as possible acquisitions at Sokol's request.

Sokol was the chief scout on this deal hunt. Like all of Warren's deals, it was to be fast and friendly. Sokol met with Lubrizol's chief executive, James Hambrick, in January 2011 to discuss the corporate culture at the two companies, and told him that a Berkshire purchase offer would be contingent on Hambrick's agreeing to stay on as CEO. After Hambrick and his board agreed to move forward with merger talks, Warren took the lead, the filing said.

While Sokol was slippery, Warren is on solid footing with Hambrick. "The company has had an outstanding record since James Hambrick became CEO in 2004, with pre-tax profits increasing from $147 million to $1,085 million," Warren wrote in the 2011 letter to shareholders.

Warren predicted that Lubrizol would have many opportunities for "bolt-on" deals in the specialty chemical field. Indeed, he has already agreed to three that Hambrick brought to the table, an investment of another $493 million in 2011 alone.

Fear Shows Up

One of the most dangerous moments in the deal process is right before the deal is decided.

The reason it's dangerous is that the discussion is no longer about which of the potential providers will be selected. That decision has been made. Even if you are in a scenario in which you are the only company proposing, your risk is still very great. You are no longer competing against one of your peers. You are competing with the prospects themselves. Let us explain.

The number one competitor to win on major sales deals in 2008 was the competitor named "Do Nothing." You may want to point to the economy as the driver for this, but in fact, this competitor has been gaining on all other competitors for the past *10 years*.

=== WARREN WAY 92 ===

Don't Do Deals Just to Do Deals

Buffett says, "We don't get paid for activity, just for being right."

When companies or even individual prospects are considering making a major buying decision, there are always four flavors of Do Nothing you may be competing against:

1. Do nothing ever
2. Do this later
3. Do something smaller
4. Do something completely different

Fear drives all of these options. And your "new competitor" is internally positioned, is politically strong, and probably offers a financial advantage that you don't. Companies delay, take half measures, and "go in a different direction" after a thorough review of solutions *all the time*. Why? Because one of these three fears won out in the decision-making process:

1. Fear of making a mistake

2. Fear of wasting money

3. Fear of losing face within the organization for not achieving a result

Because of these fears, the company and your prospects decide to do something else. To get the deal done during this most vulnerable period, you need to build all the fear killers you can into your solution. Then you need to revisit these points with your prospects and your champion throughout the closing process so that when the final decision is made, the fear is off the table and the prospects move forward with your proposed solution.

Here Are the Fear Killers

Chasm of Change

When you propose a solution to prospects, they are usually able to understand their current state, which represents the mess they are in now. They may believe in your proposed future state, which is the great benefit you have proposed in your approach. However, the thoroughness of your solution in terms of how they get from here to there will determine whether they are willing to actually take the necessary steps to buy your proposal and move forward now.

In your solutions, discussions, and presentations, you need to be crystal clear on how your company will take them across this "chasm of change," the time and effort required to get them from the current state to the future state. This means the steps, the roles and responsibilities, the timing, and the milestone measurements that let them know at each step that success is occurring and that it is safe to move forward. You cannot be too detailed in this process definition.

Tiger Team

A clear definition of the roles of the prospect's team and your team in the process, giving the responsibilities of each person at each step, gives your prospects a sense of control that makes them more comfortable in moving forward. This is especially true if one of your benefits is that you "handle everything for you." This is supposed to make your client feel great—you are going to make people's lives easier.

However, during the transition and as you are working together, there needs to be a sense of how the two companies will interface and resolve issues. For big deals, your prospects have had too many bad experiences with "set it and forget it" solutions. Create a clear picture for them of what they will be doing (such as receiving a quarterly update report) that gives them a better sense of what working together will really be like.

Slippery Slope

Show the incremental milestones with measures so that even though the deal is a big one, they can enter the water at the shallow end and get comfortable with the temperature rather than just diving into the deep end. Don't misunderstand. We are not advocating that you sell a small deal to get the promise of a larger deal later. Sell the whole deal, but show the path to the deep end in increments that they can see. We call this the "slippery slope" because as the prospects take each step, their comfort should go up and the speed of full implementation should increase. This is all based on the assumption that your company can deliver on your promises.

The key principle here is that if you do not anticipate and address your prospects' "immediately upon purchase" fears, they will take one of the other choices available to them—like doing nothing.

Winning Doesn't Mean the Game Is Over

You got the deal! Congratulations! You're set, right?

Only a rookie believes that.

You have the clawback efforts of the incumbent vendors, the fears of the internal staff, and the normal bumps and bruises of a new client relationship to work your way through.

Receiving the award is the second most dangerous part of the whole closing process. Here is what to do:

Move Fast

An old Irish toast includes the line, "and may you be a half-hour in heaven before the devil knows you're gone." This is the theme of bringing on a new deal.

You need to move the schedule you put forth in your solution very quickly. This should include peer-to-peer conversations immediately at the point of award. If you have to invent reasons to connect, exchange information, and develop relationships, *do it*.

The devil is in the area, and you need to keep him at bay. Specifically, you do not want there to be prospect's remorse or a slowing down of the deal. These things often happen right after the award phase. "Yes" doesn't mean yes until you are doing big business and the prospect is paying big invoices.

Manage Expectations

You need to reconnect with your champion and the other members of the prospect's team at the point of award. Review the timeline, the milestones, the tiger team roles and responsibilities, and any foreseeable bumps that may occur in the process of initiating this new agreement. You have been awarded the business, but that doesn't

---

WARREN WAY 100

Put Away the Rose-Colored Glasses.

Be optimistic about deal making, but be realistic, too. From *The Essays of Warren Buffett*: "In the production of rosy scenarios, Wall Street can hold its own against Washington." Hope for the best, but prepare for the worst in your deal.

THE LAST STEP IS ALWAYS SLIPPERY   [159]

mean that your prospect's team is focused on the issues of what implementation will require. You are the party that is responsible for driving the deal and keeping everyone on track.

Overcommunicate

No one is watching this deal as closely as you are. This means that you need to be the feedback loop between the prospects and the key people in your own company. The risk is found in the words, "I thought they knew that... ." We have heard these words hundreds of times in deals that were going south. The belief was the client was watching the details of the deal with the same vigilance we were.

Another belief is that when we sent the reports, invoices, and updates, the prospects were reading them with the same rigor with which we were reading them. *Not true.* The client has moved on and is going about her normal life. Once there is an award, the communication has to go up, even though the client may not be as engaged. The people on the client's team have stopped being engaged because this process took a lot of effort and they have other projects.

People won't remember their disengagement when this deals starts to flounder. They will just put the blame on you. That is why you have to overcommunicate.

Back-Channel Everything

You must hold on to your executive sponsor. Your champion is every bit as important after the award as he was before the award. There will be bumps and bruises along the way. Both during the initial stages and throughout the engagement, you need to make certain that you are preserving that voice of support.

Also, you need to gauge the internal level of satisfaction with the relationship. Too many times, a company trusts what it hears about how things are going from its day-to-day contacts every day, only to be called on the carpet by an angry client. At this point, you are stuck backing up and trying to explain. Not a good place to be.

The award is the beginning of another process, not the end of the closing process. You have to anticipate what that process will take if you want to keep and maximize your next big Warren Buffett deal.

Buffett Bonus | **Be Wary of Greed and Fear**

Buffett's famous graduate school mentor, Professor Ben Graham of Columbia University, helped him understand the folly of stock market fluctuations. Every day, investors make a deal with the stock market, deciding whether they should buy, sell, or hold. The speculative consequences are the result of two of people's most powerful emotions: greed and fear. These emotions are what cause stock prices to gyrate far above and far below the company's intrinsic value. The same is true in deal making. Buffett speaks out on the need to think independently and use sound judgment. "Once you have ordinary intelligence, what you need is the temperament to control the urges that get other people into trouble in investing," said Buffett.

LESSON 18

After You Make Your First
Warren Buffett Deal

D AIRY QUEEN was not Warren's first or biggest deal, but it may have left the best taste in his mouth.

"There's excitement when a Dairy Queen location opens in a community," said John Gainor, president and CEO of International Dairy Queen, Inc. (IDQ) in 2012. "Everyone has a story to share about his or her DQ experience."

Like the time someone allegedly saw Warren Buffett treating his friend Bill Gates to an ice cream at an Omaha Dairy Queen, and paying using a coupon.

When Warren was growing up in the 1940s and 1950s, Dairy Queens were becoming iconic fixtures of the social scene throughout the Midwest and South.

The soft serve ice cream formula was first developed in 1938 by J. F. (Grandpa) McCullough and his son Alex. They convinced a friend and customer, Sherb Noble, to offer the product in his ice cream store in Joliet, Illinois. Noble and the McCulloughs went on to open the first Dairy Queen store in 1940.

Dairy Queen was an early pioneer of food franchising, expanding its 10 stores in 1941 to 100 by 1947, 1,446 in 1950, and 2,600 in

1955. Dairy Queen went international in 1953 when the first store in Canada opened in Saskatchewan.

As Warren wrote in the 1997 letter to shareholders, for many of the intervening years, "Dairy Queen had a bumpy history. Then, in 1970, a Minneapolis group led by John Mooty and Rudy Luther took control. The new managers inherited a jumble of different franchising agreements, along with some unwise financing arrangements that had left the company in a precarious condition."

During the 25 years that followed, the new management revitalized the operation, extended food service to many more locations, and, in general, built a strong organization. But the death of one of the partners led to IDQ's being up for sale in 1997.

"Dairy Queen is a business that I like, run by an outstanding management team. Dairy Queen will be a great addition to the Berkshire family," said Warren when the deal went down. Here is how he described solving a big problem with the deal in his 1997 letter to shareholders.

Last summer Mr. Luther died, which meant his estate needed to sell stock. A year earlier, Dick Kiphart of William Blair & Co., had introduced me to John Mooty and Mike Sullivan, IDQ's CEO, and I had been impressed with both men. So, when we got the chance to merge with IDQ, we offered a proposition patterned on our FlightSafety acquisition, extending selling shareholders the option of choosing either cash or Berkshire shares having a slightly lower immediate value. By tilting the consideration as we did, we encouraged holders to opt for cash, the type of payment we by far prefer. Even then, only 45% of IDQ shares elected cash.

Charlie and I bring a modicum of product expertise to this transaction: He has been patronizing the Dairy Queens in Cass Lake and Bemidji, Minnesota, for decades, and I have been a regular in Omaha. We have put our money where our mouth is.

When the deal was done, Warren had obtained a company with 5,792 Dairy Queen stores, operating in 23 countries (all but a handful of them run by franchisees), and in addition, International Dairy Queen franchised 409 Orange Julius operations and 43 Karmelkorn operations.

How has Dairy Queen fared as part of the Berkshire Hathaway family of companies? In 2011, International Dairy Queen opened 272 new locations and hired approximately 5,000 new employees. Dairy Queen opened restaurants for the first time in 34 new cities domestically, and in Saudi Arabia, Egypt, Guatemala, and Singapore internationally.

In addition, 204 restaurants in the United States and Canada were remodeled. From 2004 to 2011, the Dairy Queen system in the United States and Canada invested nearly $800 million in opening more than 1,000 new locations and remodeling nearly 1,000. While the southern United States was the strongest market for growth, the strongest international market was China, where the Dairy Queen system opened its 500th location.

While the Oreo Blizzard is the number one seller in the United States, the Green Tea Blizzard Treat is the top seller in China. The ice cream maker, which has more than $3.2 billion in annual sales, also has more than 270 stores in Thailand.

Gainor predicted that the positive growth trend would continue. "We are projecting significant growth internationally, particularly in China," he says. "Also, in the United States and Canada, there is a tremendous opportunity for us to continue growing this brand. It is one of the most beloved brands and our customers are passionate and loyal."

Just ask Warren, one of Dairy Queen's best customers.

How Will Your Life Change?

After you make your next Warren Buffett big deal, what will have changed in your life? Certainly you and your company will have more money, and your company may have expanded greatly to keep up with the deal. But other changes will have occurred also, the changes that will make you view your professional life from a different angle.

Your horizon will have broadened in a number of ways:

1. You now think of deal making in terms of what a prospect needs. You know that your biggest deals will be about them, not you.

2. You've discovered the wonderful world of saying no. You say no to the following kinds of situations:

- The endless meetings with prospects that go nowhere
- The deal you spent an entire year pursuing when you had suspicions right from the start that you weren't going to land it
- The meetings where the head prospect is absent
- The relentless requests for more data, more samples, more examples, different pricing, and so on

3. You aren't thinking of making deals the way you used to, before your last Warren Buffett kind of deal. Let us tell you a story about this one. We have a client with whom we've worked closely for a number of years. When we started our journey, he was landing deals that were worth just under $1 million. He wanted bigger deals; his company had the capability to handle them, and he was raring to go. His first big deal was $30 million. Do you think that after that, he went back to hunting $500,000 to $1 million deals every day? Of course he didn't. His regular deal size is now $10 million, and he's currently after a $50 million deal.

=== WARREN WAY 101 ===

Predicting the Future

Buffett: "In the business world, the rearview mirror is always clearer than the windshield." Nobody knows for certain what is going to happen down the road.

---

4. You've developed an enhanced self-image.
- You have much more confidence.
- You don't sweat the small stuff anymore, and you roll with the punches easily.
- You're much more aware of others' viewpoints and ideas.
- You're not afraid to try risky and innovative approaches, ideas, and methods.
- You feel—and are—more in control of the entire sales process.
- You're finding joy in your chosen profession.

5. You've transformed your professional life.
- You're now dedicating 50 percent or more of your time to selling large accounts.
- You have developed a lively, productive team with your coworkers and others.
- You now spend at least one-quarter to one-third of your time in research.
- You've realigned your day-to-day schedule to give you blocks of time.
- You've learned to respond to prospects' needs at the CEO level in the company.
- You now rehearse your presentations many times before giving them.

And in Closing

We don't intend this book to be one that can be read quickly and absorbed thoroughly. It's not that kind of book. But then again, hunting and landing your next big Warren Buffett deal are not activities that you can wake up one morning and decide to do, without your having given them any prior thought.

This book outlines a total transformation of your business, including your buyers, your solution, your approach, your mindset, and your financial return. It doesn't happen overnight. And it's not easy to think about thoroughly in one reading, either.

After you've read through the book, we suggest that you go back and take it chapter by chapter. Mark it up. Write in the margins. Use it as a workbook, and think about how to apply the lessons. It'll take a while to do what's suggested, but do it anyway.

We have seen the methods and principles inspired by Warren Buffett and given to you in this book work time and time again as our clients have achieved the explosive growth that happens when you go after large key accounts.

And what should you do after you make your first Warren Buffett deal? Why, make your second one, of course.

Buffett Bonus | Dealmaker's Road Map for the Warren Way

Go big. Target the big deals that will make a difference.

Consider many, like some, love few. Have a deal filter that will guide your deal making.

Bad deals at good prices are still bad deals. Beware of deals that are hiding in bargain clothing but that will eat you alive.

Deal only with dealmakers. Don't waste your time dealing with people who can't make decisions.

The language of big deals. The words that are magical are money, time, and risk.

Clear the deal path. Big deals take effort, and sometimes that means removing roadblocks.

Get to dealmakers. Use the right tools to get in front of the people who can make a deal happen.

When you are going to eat an elephant, don't nibble. Don't strike with half measures; take a team to get the job done.

A little help goes a long way. Use your network to find deals and vouch for you.

Victory favors the ready. When the opportunity comes along, move fast to make a deal happen.

The why matters. Understanding why a deal makes sense to the other person might be the most important piece of information to uncover.

Expect the unexpected. Be ready to recover from a broken play.

Don't fight, but when you do . . . . Fight to get the deal back on track. Fighting is risky and should be done only as a last resort.

If you want to marry, don't tarry. Time kills deals, so do what it takes to get the deal done swiftly.

The final hour. Be on your guard when it seems that the deal is all but done.

The last step is always slippery. The deal making is never over until it is over.

101 Warren Ways

Warren Way 1. *Opportunity attracts money.* "Money will always flow toward opportunity, and there is an abundance of that in America," Buffett told his stockholders in 2011.

Warren Way 2. *How to choose deals.* Buffett to the *Wall Street Journal*: "It's like when you marry a girl. Is it her eyes? Her personality? It's a whole bunch of things you can't separate."

Warren Way 3. *Integrity matters.* "Somebody once said that in looking for people to hire, you look for three qualities: integrity, intelligence and energy," Buffett told the *Omaha World-Herald*, long before he purchased the newspaper in 2011. "And if they don't have the first, the other two will kill you."

Warren Way 4. *Avoid risky deals.* "We've done better by avoiding dragons rather than by slaying them," says Buffett.

Warren Way 5. *On choosing deals.* "I want to be in businesses so good that even a dummy can make money," Buffett told *Fortune* magazine in 1988.

Warren Way 6. *On price.* Buffett is widely quoted as saying: "It's far better to buy a wonderful company at a fair price than a fair company at a wonderful price."

Warren Way 7. *Investment criteria in a nutshell.* Here are Buffett's views from his 1996 annual report. "Your goal as an investor should be simply to purchase, at a rational price, a part interest in an easily understood business whose earnings are virtually certain to be materially higher, five, ten and twenty years from now. Over time, you will find only a few companies that meet those standards—so when you see one that qualifies, you should buy a meaningful amount of stock." Or in Buffett's case, make a deal for the whole company.

Warren Way 8. *Don't let your deal-making reach exceed your grasp.* "I don't try to jump over seven-foot bars: I look around for one-foot bars that I can step over," says Buffett.

Warren Way 9. *Have the discipline of Ted Williams.* From *The Essays of Warren Buffett:* "We try to exert a Ted Williams kind of discipline. In his book *The Science of Hitting*, Ted explained that he carved the strike zone into 77 cells, each the size of a baseball. Swinging only at balls in his 'best' cell, he knew, would allow him to hit .400; reaching for balls in his 'worst' spot, the low outside corner of the strike zone, would reduce him to .230. In other words, waiting for the fat pitch would be a trip to the Hall of Fame; swinging indiscriminately would mean a ticket to the minors."

Warren Way 10. *Don't confuse price and value.* "Price is what you pay. Value is what you get."

Warren Way 11. *Valuing a deal.* "Valuing a business is part art and part science."

Warren Way 12. *Be wary of advice.* "Never ask the barber if you need a haircut."

Warren Way 13. *Don't mindlessly imitate.* "You have to think for yourself. It always amazes me how high-IQ people mindlessly imitate. I never get good ideas talking to other people."

Warren Way 14. *Know the language of business accounting.* "When managers want to get across the facts of the business to you, it can be done within the rules of accounting. Unfortunately, when they want to play games, at least in some industries, it can also be done within the rules of accounting."

Warren Way 15. *High IQ isn't everything.* "You should have a knowledge of how business operates and the language of business [accounting], some enthusiasm for your subject, and qualities of temperament, which may be more important than IQ points."

Warren Way 16. *Hunting big deals.* Author Janet Lowe reported in *Warren Buffett Speaks* that on a 2002 trip to Britain, Buffett told the U.K. *Sunday Telegraph* that he was looking for a "big deal" in that country. "We are hunting elephant.... We have got an elephant gun and it's loaded."

Warren Way 17. *Think big or go home.* At the beginning of an annual stockholders' meeting, Buffett tapped the microphone to see if it was on: "testing... one million... two million... three million."

Warren Way 18. *Buffett admires frugality.* "Whenever I read about some company undertaking a cost-cutting program, I know it's not a company that really knows what costs are all about. Spurts don't work in this area. The really good manager does not wake up in the morning and say, 'This is the day I'm going to cut costs,' any more than he wakes up and decides to practice breathing."

Warren Way 19. *Deal making is a no-called-strike game.* Buffett says, "You don't have to swing at everything—you can wait for your pitch." Buffett is fond of baseball and often uses the game to illustrate his philosophy. In deal making, you get to stand at the plate all day, and you never have to swing. Sometimes the best deals are the ones you don't make.

Warren Way 20. *On patience and baseball.* "I've never swung at a ball while it's still in the pitcher's glove."

Warren Way 21. *Change is unavoidable.* "It's no fun being a horse when the tractor comes along, or the blacksmith when the car comes along."

Warren Way 22. *Choose quality.* "It's far better to own a portion of the Hope diamond than 100 percent of a rhinestone."

Warren Way 23. *Mediocre works too.* "Never count on making a good sale," says Buffett. "Have the purchase price be so attractive that even a mediocre sale gives good results."

Warren Way 24. *Management is key.* "Management changes, like marital changes, are painful, time-consuming, and chancy."

Warren Way 25. *To thine own self be true.* Think for yourself, and don't get caught up in the herd mentality. "Would you rather be the world's greatest lover and have everyone think that you are the world's worst lover? Or would you rather be the world's worst lover and have everyone think that you are the world's best lover?" Warren Buffett has spent his life going against the herd.

Warren Way 26. *Passion matters.* Deal only with those who believe in their products and services. "I don't want to be on the other side of the table from the customer. I was never selling anything that I didn't believe in myself or use myself."

Warren Way 27. *You can't make a good deal with a bad person.* Every deal that Buffett makes is sealed with a handshake. Then the lawyers come in and memorialize the details. If you are closing a deal with a bad person, there is no contract in the world that will protect you.

Warren Way 28. *Honesty is the best policy.* "We also believe candor benefits us as managers: The CEO who misleads others in public may eventually mislead himself in private."

Warren Way 29. *Plan for rough roads ahead.* "The roads of business are riddled with potholes; a plan that requires dodging them all is a plan for disaster."

Warren Way 30. *Nobody's perfect.* Don't expect perfection from those you are making deals with or from yourself. Be willing to make mistakes now and then. Warren said, "I make plenty of mistakes and I'll make plenty more mistakes, too. That's part of the game. You've just got to make sure that the right things overcome the wrong ones."

Warren Way 31. *Learn from others.* Buffett credits many people whom he has learned from along the way, such as his professor at Columbia Business School, Ben Graham, and his partner at Berkshire Hathaway, Charlie Munger. "You don't have to think of everything. It was Isaac Newton who said, 'I've seen a little more in the world because I stood on the shoulders of giants.' There is nothing wrong with standing on other people's shoulders."

Warren Way 32. *Research deals carefully.* In 1994, Buffett said: "Look for the durability of the franchise. The most important thing to me is figuring out how big a moat there is around the business. What I love, of course, is a big castle and a big moat with piranhas and crocodiles."

Warren Way 33. *Top two rules.* "Rule No. 1: Never lose money. Rule No. 2: Never forget rule No. 1."

Warren Way 34. *Character counts.* "When you have able managers of high character running businesses about which they are passionate, you can have a dozen or more reporting to you and still have time for an afternoon nap."

Warren Way 35. *Beware the pathology of many big deals.* The *Harvard Business Review* reported on a 1994 letter to Berkshire Hathaway shareholders in which Buffett commented on the ego of big deals. "Some years back, a CEO friend of mine—in jest, it must be said—unintentionally described the pathology of many big deals. The friend, who ran a property-casualty insurer, was explaining to his directors why he wanted to acquire a certain life insurance company. After droning rather unpersuasively through the economics and strategic rationale for the acquisition, he abruptly abandoned the script. With an impish look, he simply said, 'Aw, fellas, all the other kids have one.'"

Warren Way 36. *Research isn't everything.* "If past history was all there was to the game, the richest people would be librarians."

Warren Way 37. *Don't think computers can do your thinking for you.* "Beware of geeks bearing formulas."

Warren Way 38. *Don't adopt sloppy deal-making habits.* "Chains of habit are too light to be felt until they are too heavy to be broken."

Warren Way 39. *To the dealmaker goes the rewards.* "I don't have a problem with guilt about money. The way I see it is that my money represents an enormous number of claim checks on society. It's like I have these little pieces of paper that I can turn into consumption."

Warren Way 40. *Invest in the company that you keep.* "It's better to hang out with people better than you. Pick out associates whose behavior is better than yours and you'll drift in that direction."

Warren Way 41. *Every deal must be penciled out in advance.* "You ought to be able to explain why you're taking the job you're taking, why you're making the investment you're making, or whatever it may be. And if you can't stand applying pencil to paper, you'd better think it through some more. And if you can't write an intelligent answer to those questions, don't do it."

Warren Way 42. *There is risk in every deal.* "Risk is part of God's game, alike for men and nations."

Warren Way 43. *Premium had better mean special.* "Your premium brand had better be delivering something special," warns Buffett, "or it's not going to get the business."

Warren Way 44. *Seek simplicity in deals.* Don't overcomplicate agreements. "The business schools reward difficult complex behavior more than simple behavior, but simple behavior is most effective."

Warren Way 45. *Deal making shouldn't be difficult.* "There seems to be some perverse human characteristic that likes to make easy things difficult."

Warren Way 46. *Be ready, but don't force deals.* "You do things when the opportunities come along. I've had periods in my life when I've had a bundle of opportunities come along, and I've had long dry spells. If I get an idea next week, I'll do something. If not, I won't do a damn thing."

Warren Way 47. *All it takes is a few right deals.* "You only have to do a very few things right in your life so long as you don't do too many things wrong."

Warren Way 48. *Don't overleverage yourself.* "Only when the tide goes out do you discover who has been swimming naked."

Warren Way 49. *Beware the G-word in deal making.* "I will tell you how to become rich. Close the doors. Be fearful when others are greedy. Be greedy when others are fearful."

Warren Way 50. *Make deals in areas you understand.* In 2008, Buffett was asked by CNBC about his interest in making a deal with candy giants Wrigley and Mars. "Well, I understand a Wrigley or a Mars a whole lot better than I understand the balance sheet of some of the big banks. I know what I'm getting in this, and some of the larger financial institutions, I really don't know what's there."

Warren Way 51. *Take a long-term view when you make a deal.* Buffett likes the adage: "Someone is sitting in the shade today because someone planted a tree a long time ago."

Warren Way 52. *Deals can take time.* "No matter how great the talent or efforts, some things just take time. You can't produce a baby in one month by getting nine women pregnant."

Warren Way 53. *Sellers of a business beware.* From *The Essays of Warren Buffett:* "Most business owners spend the better part of their lifetimes building their businesses... In contrast, owner-managers sell their business only once—frequently in an emotionally-charged atmosphere with a multitude of pressures coming from different directions."

Warren Way 54. *Sometimes all you have to do is show up.* When he was in college, Buffett read an item in the school newspaper that said that a $500 graduate school scholarship was to be awarded that day. Applicants should go to Room 300, and they could earn a scholarship to the accredited school of the student's choice. "I went to Room 300 and I was the only guy who showed up. The three professors there kept wanting to wait. I said, 'No, no. It was three o'clock.' So I won the scholarship without doing anything."

Warren Way 55. *Pick your battles.* Buffett learned this during his dealings with Salomon. "I could have fought harder and been more vocal. I might have felt better about myself if I did. But it wouldn't have changed the course of history. Unless you sort of enjoy combat, it doesn't make sense."

Warren Way 56. *Focus.* Focus. Focus. From the biography *The Snowball* comes this tale from the day in 1991 when Buffett met and spent the Fourth of July with Bill Gates and his family. Buffett recalls: "Then at dinner, Bill Gates Sr. posed the question to the table: What factor did people feel was the most important in getting to where they'd gotten in life? And I said 'Focus,' and Bill [Bill Gates Jr.] said the same thing."

Warren Way 57. *Get your facts straight.* "And the truth is, you are neither right nor wrong because people agree with you. You're right because your facts are right and reasoning right. In the end, that's what counts."

Warren Way 58. *Don't compromise on your career.* Don't waste time with your time or your life. When it comes to your career, go for the deals you really want. "It's crazy to take little in-between jobs just because they look good on your resume. That's like saving sex for your old age."

Warren Way 59. *Definition of an ideal business.* This is what Buffett looks for when he seeks a business to obtain. "The ideal business is one that earns very high returns on capital and that keeps using lots of capital at those high returns. That becomes a compounding machine."

Warren Way 60. *Love is the greatest return.* From the Buffett biography *The Snowball*: "That's the ultimate test of how you have lived your life. The trouble with love is you can't buy it. You can buy sex. You can buy testimonial dinners. You can buy pamphlets that say how wonderful you are. But the only way to get love is to be lovable."

Warren Way 61. *Share the profits with your key players.* Rock superstar Bono of U2 asked for 15 minutes of Buffett's time at a corporate event. "I love music. But actually U2's music doesn't blow me away. What interests me is that Bono splits the revenue of U2 among four people absolutely equally."

Warren Way 62. *Set aside reserves for when deals go bad.* "You absolutely never want to be in a position where tomorrow morning you have to depend on the kindness of strangers in the financial world. I spent a lot of time thinking about that. I never want to have to come up with a billion dollars tomorrow morning. Well, a billion I could."

Warren Way 63. *Have a little cash in reserve.* "Cash combined with courage in a time of crisis is priceless."

Warren Way 64. *On good deal making and the snowballing effect.* People from Nebraska know about snow and how to make snowballs. From the biography *The Snowball*: "The snowball just happens if you're in the right kind of snow, and that's what happened with me. I don't mean just compounding money either. It's in terms of understanding the world and what types of friends you accumulate. You get to select over time, and you've got to be the kind of person that the snow wants to attach itself to. You've got to be your own wet snow, in effect. You'd better be picking up snow as you go along, because you're not going to be getting back up to the top of the hill again. That's the way life works."

Warren Way 65. *Think for yourself.* In graduate school, Buffett was amazed at how other students were willing to go with the flow of conventional wisdom. "I don't think there was one person in the class that thought about whether U.S. Steel was a good business. I mean, it was a big business, but they weren't thinking about what kind of train they were getting on."

Warren Way 66. *Price isn't the be-all and end-all.* From *The Essays of Warren Buffett:* "Price is very important, but often is not the most critical aspect of the sale." Buffett looks hard at people issues and the terms of the deal.

Warren Way 67. *Know the true value.* In 1973, the market price for the Washington Post Company was $80 million, and the company had no debt. Buffett uses this as an example of a great deal. "If you asked anyone in the business what [the *Post*'s] properties were worth, they'd have said $400 million or something like that. You could have an auction in the middle of the Atlantic Ocean at 2:00 in the morning, and you would have had people show up and bid that much for them. And it was being run by honest and able people who all had a significant part of their net worth in the business. It was ungodly safe. It wouldn't have bothered me to put my whole net worth in it. Not in the least."

Warren Way 68. *Judging humans is imperfect at best.* "There is no way to eliminate the possibility of error when judging humans."

Warren Way 69. *No bluffing.* No kidding. "We don't bluff. It's not my style anyway. Over a lifetime, you'll get a reputation for either bluffing or not bluffing. And therefore, I want it to be understood that I don't do it."

Warren Way 70. *No pressure.* "People tell me I put pressure on them. I never intend to. Some people like to apply pressure. I never do. It's actually the last thing I like to do."

Warren Way 71. *Match your people to your principles.* "I said we would have people to match our principles, rather than the reverse," Buffett once mused. "But I found out that wasn't so easy."

Warren Way 72. *Know what deals work for you and then focus on those deals.* From *The Essays of Warren Buffett*: "Charlie [Munger] and I frequently get approached about acquisitions that don't come close to meeting our tests: We've found that if you advertise an interest in buying collies, a lot of people will call hoping to sell you their cocker spaniels. A line from a country song expresses our feeling about new ventures, turnarounds, or auction-like sales: 'When the phone don't ring, you'll know it's me.'"

Warren Way 73. *Give something back when the dealing's done.* "What better can you do with money," Buffett told *USA Today*, "than to help thousands of people change their lives in a very, very positive way?"

Warren Way 74. *Support success.* "I like to back success," Warren told *USA Today* in 2012. "I like things that change people's lives."

Warren Way 75. *Think long term.* "Our favorite holding period is forever."

Warren Way 76. *Folly is your deal-making friend.* Economic fluctuations create motivated sellers who are willing to discount. "Profit from folly rather than participate in it."

Warren Way 77. *You can't hurry love or deals.* From *The Essays of Warren Buffett*: "In the search, we adopt the same attitude one might find appropriate in looking for a spouse: It pays to be active, interested, and open-minded, but it does not pay to be in a hurry."

Warren Way 78. *Deals begin at home.* Buffett encourages his shareholders to buy from company-owned businesses. "Remember," he told shareholders at the annual meeting, "anyone who says money can't buy happiness simply hasn't learned where to shop."

Warren Way 79. *Cash in and out determines value.* From *The Essays of Warren Buffett*: "In *Theory of Investment Value*, written over 50 years ago, John Burr Williams set forth the equation for value, which we condense here: *The value of any stock, bond or business today* *is determined by the cash inflows and outflows—discounted at an appropriate interest rate—that can be expected to occur during the lifetime of the asset."*

Warren Way 80. *On the future of deal making.* "Human potential is far from exhausted, and the American system for unleashing that potential—a system that has worked wonders over two centuries despite frequent interruptions for recessions and even a Civil War—remains alive and effective."

Warren Way 81. *It's never too soon to be talking about money.* As told in *The Essays of Warren Buffett,* Buffett is crystal clear on what he is looking for when he looks for companies: "An offering price (we don't want to waste our time or that of the seller by talking, even preliminarily, about a transaction when price is unknown)."

Warren Way 82. *Be wary of projections.* In 1982 Warren said, "While deals often fail in practice, they never fail in projections."

Warren Way 83. *Don't trust financial projections.* From *The Essays of Warren Buffett:* Why potential buyers put much stock in financial projections baffles Buffett, but he keeps in mind the story of the man with an ailing horse. "Visiting the vet, he said: 'Can you help me? Sometimes my horse walks just fine and sometimes he limps.' The vet's reply was pointed. 'No problem—when he's walking fine, sell him.'"

Warren Way 84. *Be thankful for a free press.* "The smarter the journalists are, the better off society is."

Warren Way 85. *Deal what you know.* Buffett says you need to love the deals you make and leave the others alone. "There are all kinds of businesses that Charlie [Munger] and I don't understand, but that doesn't cause us to stay up at night. It just means we go on to the next one."

Warren Way 86. *Dealmakers beware.* From *The Essays of Warren Buffett:* "Talking to *Time* magazine a few years back, Peter Drucker got to the heart of things: 'I will tell you a secret: Deal making beats working. Deal making is exciting and fun, and working is grubby.

Running anything is primarily an enormous amount of grubby detail work... deal making is... romantic, sexy. That's why you have deals that make no sense.'"

Warren Way 87. *Be opportunistic.* "You do things when the opportunities come along," says Buffett.

Warren Way 88. *Do your homework.* "Risk comes from not knowing what you are doing," says Warren.

Warren Way 89. *Pay attention to trends.* Read, read, and read some more about trends that could affect your deal. In 2008, Buffett shared this story in a CNBC interview. "Well, I've got a son that's a farmer. He's a very happy fellow. They used to tell the story out here in Nebraska about the farmer that won the lottery, and they sent a television crew out to see him. And the television interviewer said, 'You know, you've just won twenty million dollars in the lottery, what are you going to do with it?' And the farmer said, 'Well, I think I'll just keep farming until it's all gone.' Well, that was the situation in farming until the last year or so, but it's a different world now." The moral of the story is pay attention to trends. Thanks to advances in fuels like ethanol, farming is as much about energy these days as it is about food.

Warren Way 90. *Marry your fortunes well.* Buffett once said: "Our situation is the opposite of Camelot's Mordred, of whom Guenevere commented, 'The one thing I can say for him is that he is bound to marry well. Everybody is above him.'"

Warren Way 91. *Dealmaker beware.* From *The Essays of Warren Buffett*: "We believe most deals do damage to the acquiring company. Too often, the words from *HMS Pinafore* apply: 'Things are seldom what they seem, skim milk masquerades as cream.' Specifically, sellers and their representatives invariably present financial projections having more entertainment value than educational value."

Warren Way 92. *Don't do deals just to do deals.* Buffett says, "We don't get paid for activity, just for being right."

Warren Way 93. *Complex calculations are not necessary.* "If calculus or algebra were required to be a great investor, I'd have to go back to delivering newspapers," admits Buffett. "I've never seen any need for algebra. Essentially, you're trying to figure out the value of a business." His uncommon gift for closing a deal is common sense. Simple mathematics and a logical brain are what you need in order to withstand the emotions of deal making, because emotions can get in the way of closing a deal.

Warren Way 94. *Keep your promises.* From *The Essays of Warren Buffett:* "When we tell John Justin that his business (Justin Industries) will remain headquartered in Fort Worth, or assure the Bridge family that its operation (Ben Bridge Jeweler) will not be merged with another jeweler, these sellers can take those promises to the bank."

Warren Way 95. *Have fun doing the deals.* "We enjoy the process far more than the proceeds."

Warren Way 96. *If you smell a bad deal, do what you can to get out gracefully.* "Should you find yourself in a chronically leaking boat, energy devoted to changing vessels is likely to be more productive than energy devoted to patching leaks."

Warren Way 97. *Invest in the deals that turn you on.* Buffett says it pays to specialize in areas that interest you. "Why not invest your assets in the companies you really like? As Mae West said, 'Too much of a good thing can be wonderful.'"

Warren Way 98. *Think for yourself.* "My idea of a group decision is to look in the mirror."

Warren Way 99. *Be honest in your deal making.* Buffett told his son Howard: "It takes 20 years to build a reputation and five minutes to ruin it. If you think about that, you'll do things differently."

Warren Way 100. *Put away the rose-colored glasses.* Be optimistic about deal making, but be realistic, too. From *The Essays of Warren Buffett:* "In the production of rosy scenarios, Wall Street can hold its own against Washington." Hope for the best, but prepare for the worst in your deal.

Warren Way 101. *Predicting the future.* Buffett: "In the business world, the rearview mirror is always clearer than the windshield." Nobody knows for certain what is going to happen down the road.

Chronology of Buffett Deal Highlights

1962. Buffett begins buying stock in *Berkshire Hathaway*, apparently noticing a stock price pattern each time the company closed a mill. Eventually, he concedes that the textile business is a declining industry and that the company's fortunes will not improve. He has a chance to sell his holdings, but he rejects the offer as a result of a dispute over price ($11.38 versus $11.50 a share), gains control of the company, and fires the principal. Becoming the majority owner of a failing textile company because of a perceived slight over price, Buffett says later, was the biggest investment mistake he has ever made. Had the additional money that he poured into Berkshire been invested in the insurance business for 45 years instead, he calculates that it would have produced several hundred times the results.

1966. Buffett makes his first investment in a private business, *Hochschild, Kohn & Co.*, a privately owned Baltimore department store.

1967. Buffett buys insurer *National Indemnity* in a cash transaction.

1970. Buffett contacts the owner of the *Washington Post Company*, Katharine Graham, to tell her that he is acquiring a substantial number of shares of the newspaper company, but that he is not planning a hostile takeover.

1972. Buffett sticks to his guns and buys *See's Candies* for $25 million, although the buyer was holding out for $5 million more. The chocolate maker's revenues are seasonal, with half of them coming in November and December. The cash flow from See's provides the capital for many future purchases.

1973. Buffett begins acquiring stock in the *Washington Post Company*.

1977. Buffett buys the *Buffalo Evening News* and resumes publication of a Sunday edition that had ceased in 1914. A competitor folds in 1982. Tellingly, Berkshire ventures into other media but generally avoids purchasing newspapers until he buys the hometown *Omaha World-Herald* in 2011.

1983. *Nebraska Furniture Mart* joins Buffett's holdings. It's a legend in Omaha, and it's run by an elderly Russian émigré who never had any formal schooling. Buffett buys a 90 percent stake for $55 million on a handshake. The émigré, Rose Blumkin, and her family stay.

1985. Berkshire purchases a major position in *Capital Cities/ABC*.

1986. *Scott Fetzer Companies* is acquired. It is a diversified group of 22 manufacturing and distribution businesses. Many people know it for its Kirby home cleaning systems, Wayne Water Systems, and Campbell Hausfeld products.

1986. Buffett buys *Fechheimer Brothers Company*, a company that makes, rents, and cleans uniforms.

1988. Buffett begins buying shares of *Coca-Cola*.

1989. Buffett closes the deal to buy *Borsheims*, a jewelry store in Omaha that is owned by the sister and brother-in-law of Rose Blumkin, the legendary Mrs. B of Nebraska Furniture Mart.

1991. Berkshire purchases *H. H. Brown*, a manufacturer of work boots and shoes.

1992. Buffett buys *Central States Indemnity*, which provides insurance for credit card payments for people who are unable to pay because of disability or unemployment.

1992. Buffett spends most of the year in New York serving as chairman of *Salomon* Brothers in the wake of illegal bond-trading activity.

1993. Berkshire buys *Dexter Shoes*, a maker of popularly priced men's and women's shoes.

1995. *Helzberg Diamonds*, a jewelry store chain based in Kansas City, is acquired.

1995. Buffett adds to Berkshire's furniture empire with the purchase of the Utah-based *RC Willey* Home Furnishings.

1996. Berkshire buys a service business. *FlightSafety International*, with headquarters in Flushing, New York, trains the operators of aircraft and ships.

1996. Berkshire's insurance holdings, which are widely recognized as Buffett's forte, gain with the addition of *GEICO*, an acronym for Government Employees Insurance Company and affiliates. The company is based in Chevy Chase, Maryland. GEICO is known for marketing policies through direct response, with applications being submitted directly to the companies.

1998. General aviation aircraft are often owned through fractional ownership programs. All of *NetJets Inc.* now belongs to Buffett's empire.

1998. Dessert, anyone? *Dairy Queen,* which services 6,000 stores under the names Dairy Queen, Orange Julius, and Karmelkorn, is acquired.

1998. Buffett's love affair with insurance companies continues. Berkshire buys *General Re*, a reinsurer with various holdings. Its operations are based in Stamford, Connecticut, and Cologne, Germany.

2000. Buffett's company buys *Ben Bridge Jeweler*, a western chain, adding to its jewelry holdings.

2000. The empire picks up *CORT Business Services*, a provider of rental furniture.

2000. Berkshire enters the building products business, acquiring brick maker *Acme Building Brands* of Texas and *Benjamin Moore & Co.* of New Jersey, which makes architectural coatings.

2001. Berkshire buys 87 percent of *Shaw Industries*, a Georgia company known as the world's largest maker of carpet and laminate flooring, and soon buys the remainder.

2001. Three more building product companies are acquired, including insulation maker *Johns Manville* and a 90 percent stake in *MiTek Inc.*, a maker of engineered connector products such as building trusses.

2002. *Albeca*, a Georgia company, is acquired. It designs, manufactures, and distributes custom picture framing products.

2002. Berkshire acquires *CTB International Corp.* The Indiana firm is a designer, manufacturer, and marketer of systems used in the grain industry.

2002. Berkshire picks up *Fruit of the Loom*, a maker of underwear, for some $850 million in cash.

2002. *Russell Corp.*, the nation's largest maker of sweatshirts and sweat pants, comes next for $600 million.

2002. *The Pampered Chef* a direct seller of kitchen tools, is purchased. The Pampered Chef has a network of 65,000 independent sales representatives.

2003. *Clayton Homes*, a vertically integrated manufactured housing company based in Knoxville, Tennessee, comes into the fold.

2003. Berkshire buys *McLane Company* from Walmart. The empire now reaches into Brazil; McLane is a distributor to discount retailers, convenience stores, and theater complexes.

2007. Berkshire acquires *Marmon Holdings* from the Pritzker family. It makes railroad tank cars, shopping carts, plumbing pipes, wiring, and water treatment products.

2007. Berkshire buys *NRG*, a Dutch life reinsurance company.

2009. In his largest acquisition to date, Buffett buys the 78 percent of *Burlington Northern Santa Fe Railway* that he does not already own. It is the nation's second-largest railroad, and its fuel efficiency is such that an average train can carry 280 truckloads. The move is seen as a bet on the economy rebounding.

2011. *Lubrizol*, a maker of engine additives, is acquired for $9.7 billion. Buffett's heir apparent, David Sokol, later resigns from Berkshire Hathaway after it is learned that he personally bought stock in advance of advising Buffett to buy the company.

The Making of a
Dealmaker

*D*EAL was a dirty word in the Buffett household when Warren was growing up in the 1930s, during the Great Depression. His father, Howard Buffett, was a conservative four-term congressman and a fierce critic of President Franklin Roosevelt's New Deal policies.

But even as a child, Warren was making deals: selling gum, magazines, and soda door to door; working in his grandfather's grocery store; delivering newspapers; and detailing cars. He filed his first income tax return at age 14. The next year, he and a buddy bought a

---

WARREN WAY 39

To the Dealmaker Goes the Rewards

"I don't have a problem with guilt about money. The way I see it is that my money represents an enormous number of claim checks on society. It's like I have these little pieces of paper that I can turn into consumption."

---

used pinball machine that they made a deal to place in a barbershop. Soon they made deals to own several machines in several shops.

WARREN WAY 54

Sometimes All You Have to Do Is Show Up

When he was in college, Buffett read an item in the school newspaper that said that a $500 graduate school scholarship was to be awarded that day. Applicants should go to Room 300, and they could earn a scholarship to the accredited school of the student's choice. "I went to Room 300 and I was the only guy who showed up. The three professors there kept wanting to wait. I said, 'No, no. It was three o'clock.' So I won the scholarship without doing anything."

While he was in high school, Buffett invested in a business owned by his father and bought a farm worked by a tenant farmer. The comment below his senior picture in the yearbook at Woodrow Wilson High in Washington, DC, read: "Likes math; a future stock broker."

Warren entered Wharton Business School at the University of Pennsylvania in 1947, transferred to the University of Nebraska at Lincoln in 1950, and graduated with a bachelor's degree in business. He enrolled at Columbia Business School after learning that security analysts Benjamin Graham (author of *The Intelligent Investor*) and David Dodd taught there. He earned a master's degree in economics in 1951 and also attended the New York Institute of Finance.

During the 1950s, Warren progressed from investment salesperson to securities analyst to general partner. Since 1970, he has been making his deals as chairman and chief executive officer of Berkshire Hathaway Inc., which is effectively his own holding company. Warren likens Berkshire to a work of art that he has spent decades creating, and says that the true measure of the company cannot be judged until he is finished.

Early Deal-Making Success

In April 1952, Warren discovered that Graham was on the board of GEICO insurance. He took a train to the company's Washington headquarters, recounts author Roger Lowenstein in *Buffett: The Making of an American Capitalist,* and convinced a janitor to let him in even though it was a Saturday. There he met Lorimer Davidson, GEICO's vice president. The two discussed the insurance business for hours, and Davidson became a lifelong friend.

When Warren graduated from Columbia, he wanted to work on Wall Street, but both his father and Graham urged him not to.

Warren liked sharing his knowledge. He returned to Omaha and worked as a stockbroker, while at the same time teaching a night class in Investment Principles at the University of Nebraska to students who typically were twice his age. Not all of his deals went well. He purchased a gas station as a side investment, but it did not turn out well.

In 1952, Warren married Susan Thompson, and the next year they

=== **WARREN WAY 2** ===

How to Choose Deals

Buffett to the *Wall Street Journal*: "It's like when you marry a girl. Is it her eyes? Her personality? It's a whole bunch of things you can't separate."

had their first child, Susan Alice. In 1954, he accepted a job in a Graham partnership for $12,000 a year (about $100,000 today). He worked closely with Walter Schloss, who was adamant that stocks must provide a wide margin of safety after weighing the trade-off between their price and their intrinsic value. Warren understood the argument but questioned whether Schloss's criteria were too stringent and caused the company to miss out on big winners that had more qualitative values. That same year, the Buffetts had their second child, Howard Graham.

By this time, Warren's personal savings had risen to more than $1 million, and he started Buffett Partnership, Ltd., in Omaha.

Warren still lives in the house he bought for $31,500 in 1957, when he had three investment partnerships operating. The next year, the Buffetts' third child, Peter Andrew, was born. The three partnerships had grown to five, and a sixth was added the next year. In one partnership, 11 doctors invested $10,000 each, but Warren invested only $100 of his own funds.

Sanborn Map Company was an example of an early deal-making success. Warren's partnership bought it in 1958 for $45 a share, calculating its true value at $65 a share. By 1961, Warren revealed that Sanborn Map Company accounted for 35 percent of the partnership's assets. Warren won a seat on Sanborn's board.

Berkshire Hathaway, Warren's Reluctant Masterpiece

Warren truly became a millionaire in 1962 through his share of the partnerships' $7.1 million in assets. He merged all the partnerships into one, then invested in and eventually took control of a textile manufacturing firm, Berkshire Hathaway, that would become his holding company. But things were not what they seemed.

WARREN WAY 91

Dealmaker Beware

From *The Essays of Warren Buffett:* "We believe most deals do damage to the acquiring company. Too often, the words from *HMS Pinafore* apply: 'Things are seldom what they seem, skim milk masquerades as cream.' Specifically, sellers and their representatives invariably present financial projections having more entertainment value than educational value."

Ironically, the Berkshire deal is not one that Warren is proud that he made. In 1962, Warren began buying stock in the company, apparently noticing a stock price pattern each time Berkshire closed a mill. His first purchases of Berkshire were at $7.60 a share, and by 1965 he was paying $14.86, although he calculated that the company had working capital of $19 a share.

Eventually, he conceded that the textile business was a declining industry and that the company's fortunes would not improve. He had a chance to sell his holdings, but he rejected the offer because of a dispute over price ($11.38 versus $11.50 a share), gained control of the company, and fired the principal. He named a new president, Ken Chace, to run the company. In 1966, Warren closed the partnership to new money. He also made his first investment in a private business—Hochschild, Kohn & Co., a Baltimore department store.

Becoming majority owner of a failing textile company because of a perceived slight over price, Warren said later, was the biggest deal-making mistake he has ever made. Had the additional money that he poured into Berkshire been invested in the insurance business for 45 years instead, he calculates that it would have produced several hundred times the results.

In 1967, Berkshire paid a dividend of 10 cents—its first and only dividend. In 1970, Warren, as chairman of Berkshire Hathaway, began writing his now-famous annual letters to shareholders, which have been packed with lessons about deal making and investing. His salary then was $50,000 a year, augmented by his outside investment income.

Another milestone was reached in 1979. Berkshire's stock began the year at $775 a share and finished at $1,310. Warren's net worth reached $620 million, placing him on the Forbes 400 list for the first time.

Warren told *BusinessWeek* in 1999, "Berkshire is my painting, so it should look the way I want it to." He also said: "There is nothing remotely as fun as running Berkshire."

Those 1970s Deals

In 1972, through his company Blue Chip Stamps, he bought the California confectionary company See's Candies. The chocolate maker's revenues are seasonal, with half coming in November and December, but they continue to rise with each holiday season. Warren says he likes a business where the answer to the question, "What shall we charge next year?" is the word "more."

Warren, the former newspaper delivery boy, began dabbling in media companies in 1973, acquiring stock in the Washington Post Company. He became close friends with the publisher, Katharine Graham, who controlled the company and its flagship newspaper, and became a member of its board of directors.

In 1974, the Securities and Exchange Commission opened a formal investigation into Warren Buffett and Berkshire's acquisition of Wesco, a small savings and loan company, because of a possible conflict of interest. No charges were brought.

The purchase of another media company, the *Buffalo Evening News*, in 1977 also prompted regulatory scrutiny. Antitrust charges

---

WARREN WAY 67

Know the True Value

In 1973, the market price for the *Washington Post* was $80 million, and the company had no debt. Buffett began buying stock and uses this as an example of a great deal. "If you asked anyone in the business what [the *Post*'s] properties were worth, they'd have said $400 million or something like that. You could have an auction in the middle of the Atlantic Ocean at 2:00 in the morning, and you would have had people show up and bid that much for them. And it was being run by honest and able people who all had a significant part of their net worth in the business. It was ungodly safe. It wouldn't have bothered me to put my whole net worth in it. Not in the least."

were started, instigated by the rival *Buffalo Courier-Express*. Both papers lost money until the *Courier-Express* folded in 1982. Berkshire then ventured into other media but generally avoided purchasing newspapers until it bought the hometown *Omaha World-Herald* in 2011.

In 1979, Berkshire began buying stock in ABC. Capital Cities, just one-fourth the size of ABC, shocked the investment world with a $3.5 billion purchase offer in 1985. Warren helped finance the deal in return for a 25 percent stake in the combined company. Another regulatory issue, duplication in some markets, forced the newly merged company to sell off some radio stations.

The Go-Go 1980s

As a present to himself, Warren bought the Nebraska Furniture Mart on his fifty-third birthday in 1983. The store was a legend in his native Omaha, run by an elderly Russian émigré who had never had any formal schooling. Warren bought a 90 percent stake for $55 million on a handshake. The émigré, Rose Blumkin, and her family stayed on as partners.

In 1986, Warren made a deal to acquire Scott Fetzer Companies, a diversified group of 22 manufacturing and distribution businesses. Many people know it for its Kirby home cleaning systems, Wayne Water Systems, and Campbell Hausfeld products.

Not all of Warren's acquisitions went smoothly. In 1987, Berkshire purchased a 12 percent stake in Salomon Inc., making it the largest shareholder, and Warren became a director. In 1990, a scandal involving John Gutfreund (the CEO of Salomon Brothers at the time) surfaced. A rogue trader was submitting bids in excess of what the Treasury rules allowed, and when Gutfreund learned about it, he failed to suspend the individual immediately. Gutfreund left the company in August 1991, and Warren became chairman until the crisis passed. In September 1991, Warren was called to testify before Congress.

Things went better with Coke, however. In 1988, Warren began buying stock in Coca-Cola Company, eventually purchasing 7 percent of the company for $1.02 billion. This turned out to be one of Berkshire's most lucrative investments, and one that it still holds. Warren might be the company's best customer: in 2012, *Time* reported that he drinks 60 ounces a day.

Picking Up Speed in the 1990s

While Warren had been a millionaire in 1962, he was a billionaire in 1990 when Berkshire class A shares began trading at $7,175 a share. There was a flurry of high-profile deals in the late 1990s. Helzberg Diamonds, a jewelry store chain based in Kansas City, was acquired in 1995. Then, in 1996, Berkshire bought a service business, New York–based FlightSafety International, that trains the operators of aircraft and ships.

Insurance holdings, which are widely recognized as Warren's forte, increased in 1996 with the addition of GEICO, an acronym for Government Employees Insurance Company and affiliates. Based in Chevy Chase, Maryland, GEICO is known for marketing policies through direct response, with applications being submitted directly to the companies.

In 1998, general aviation aircraft, often owned through fractional ownership programs, were added to the empire with the acquisition of NetJets Inc. Also in that year, Dairy Queen, which services 6,000 stores under the names Dairy Queen, Orange Julius, and Karmelkorn, was acquired. (Warren is fond of Dilly Bars and has been seen

=== WARREN WAY 32 ===

Research Deals Carefully

In 1994, Buffett said: "Look for the durability of the franchise. The most important thing to me is figuring out how big a moat there is around the business. What I love, of course, is a big castle and a big moat with piranhas and crocodiles."

at a Dairy Queen with various notables, including Microsoft founder Bill Gates.)

Warren understood insurance companies, but his acquisition deals did not come without grief. He acquired General Re for stock in 1998, and in 2002 he became involved with Maurice R. Greenberg at AIG, with General Re providing reinsurance. Three years later, AIG's board forced Greenberg to resign as chairman and CEO under the shadow of criticism from Eliot Spitzer, then attorney general of New York State. AIG paid a $1.6 billion fine as part of a 2006 settlement. In 2010, the federal government settled with Berkshire for $92 million, and the company made what were called "corporate governance concessions" to avoid prosecution in the AIG fraud scheme.

Berkshire's insurance businesses initially provided insurance and reinsurance of property and casualty risks primarily in the United States. With the General Re acquisition in 1998, his holdings branched out into life, accident, and health reinsurance as well as foreign insurers. Yet a common characteristic of Berkshire's insurance companies is that they maintain capital strength at exceptionally high levels.

The Good, Bad, and Ugly 2000s

In 2000 and 2001, there was another flurry of deals. In 2000, Warren made deals to obtain Ben Bridge Jeweler, a western chain, adding to its jewelry holdings; CORT Business Services, a provider of rental furniture; brick maker Acme Building Brands of Texas; and Benjamin Moore & Co. of New Jersey, a maker of paints. More deals followed in 2001: Berkshire bought 87 percent of Shaw Industries, a Georgia company known as the world's largest maker of carpet and laminate flooring, and soon bought the remainder, and three more building products companies were acquired, including insulation maker Johns Manville and a 90 percent stake in MiTek Inc., a maker of engineered connector products such as building trusses.

In 2002, Warren continued to make deals at a healthy clip: he acquired Albeca, a Georgia company that designs, manufactures, and distributes custom picture framing products. Berkshire also acquired CTB International Corp., an Indiana designer, manufacturer, and marketer of systems used in the grain industry; picked up Fruit of the Loom, a maker of underwear, for some $850 million in cash; bought Russell Corp., the nation's largest maker of sweatshirts and sweat pants, for $600 million; and finally, made a deal for the Pampered Chef, a direct seller of kitchen tools that has a network of 65,000 independent sales representatives.

Two more big deals went down in 2003. Warren bought Clayton Homes, a vertically integrated manufactured housing company based in Knoxville, Tennessee, and purchased McLane Company from Walmart.

In June 2006, having billions in wealth, Warren announced that he would give away 85 percent of his Berkshire holdings to five foundations in annual gifts of stock. The largest slice would go to the Bill and Melinda Gates Foundation.

By 2007, Warren's attention had turned to identifying a possible successor. He announced in a letter to shareholders that he was looking for a younger successor, or perhaps successors. Warren had previously selected Lou Simpson, who runs investments at GEICO, to fill that role. However, Simpson is only six years younger than Warren.

WARREN WAY 41

Every Deal Must Be Penciled Out in Advance

"You ought to be able to explain why you're taking the job you're taking, why you're making the investment you're making, or whatever it may be. And if you can't stand applying pencil to paper, you'd better think it through some more. And if you can't write an intelligent answer to those questions, don't do it."

The Great Recession

The man with the golden touch suffered along with others during the Great Recession of the late 2000s.

During the subprime crisis of 2007–2008, he was criticized for allocating capital too early, resulting in suboptimal deals. Berkshire suffered a 77 percent drop in earnings during the third quarter of 2008, and several deals after that appeared vulnerable to large mark-to-market losses, according to analysts.

As one of the world's wealthiest men, Warren played a significant role in addressing the crisis in the debt and equity markets. Berkshire acquired 10 percent perpetual preferred stock of Goldman Sachs. According to Reuters, when put options that he wrote faced $6.73 billion mark-to-market losses, the SEC demanded that his firm produce a more thorough disclosure of the factors used to value the contracts.

Warren also helped Dow Chemical pay for its $18.8 billion takeover of Rohm and Haas, with Berkshire becoming the single largest shareholder in the enlarged group after providing $3 billion in financing.

Despite the recession, Warren gained the title of richest man in the world in 2008 when his net worth by *Forbes*'s calculations reached $62 billion. He dethroned Bill Gates, who had led the *Forbes* list for 13 years. (Gates bounced back the next year when Warren's net worth declined $25 billion, according to *Forbes*.)

Still, the acquisitions continued. Notably, Warren made a deal to acquire General Electric's preferred stock.

There were second-guessers, particularly during the 2000s. Some wondered why Berkshire still held a major position in Coca-Cola when the company's stock had peaked at $86 in 1998.

Warren's response on the difficulties of knowing when to sell came in his 2004 letter: "That may seem easy to do when one looks through an always-clean, rear-view mirror. Unfortunately, however, it's the windshield through which investors must peer, and that glass is invariably fogged."

By March 2009, Warren, too, was concerned. He told an interviewer for MSN.com that the economy had "fallen off a cliff.... Not only has the economy slowed down a lot, but people have really changed their habits like I haven't seen."

But the deals kept on coming. In 2009, he invested $2.6 billion as a part of Swiss Re's raising equity capital, then, in his largest acquisition to date, Warren bought the 78 percent of Burlington Northern Santa Fe (BNSF) that he did not already own for $34 billion. BNSF is the nation's second-largest railroad, and its fuel efficiency is such that an average train can carry 280 truckloads. The move was seen as a bet on the economy rebounding. One prominent analyst viewed it as a move to diversify Berkshire Hathaway away from the financial industry.

By June 2009, Berkshire was ranked by the *Financial Times* as the eighteenth-largest corporation in the world, based on market capitalization. That year, Warren divested his failed investment in ConocoPhillips, telling Berkshire investors that he had purchased a large amount of shares when oil and gas prices were near their peak.

"I in no way anticipated the dramatic fall in energy prices that occurred in the last half of the year," said Warren. "I still believe the odds are good that oil sells far higher in the future than the current $40–$50 price. Even if prices should rise, moreover, the terrible timing of my purchase has cost Berkshire several billion dollars."

2010 and Beyond

The "Oracle of Omaha" (no Warren Buffett book is complete without trotting out that chestnut) came to the defense of credit rating agencies in June 2010 for their role in the U.S. financial crisis: "Very, very few people could appreciate the bubble. That's the nature of bubbles—they're mass delusions."

By March 2011, Goldman Sachs had received Federal Reserve approval to buy back Berkshire's preferred stock in Goldman from a reluctant Warren, who was not eager to give up $1.4 million in dividends a day.

During 2011, Warren surprised the investment world by quietly purchasing 64 million shares of International Business Machines (IBM), a 5.5 percent stake worth $11 billion—this from the man who said repeatedly that he would not invest in technology because he did not fully understand it, and who even refused Gates's offer to send a Microsoft employee to personally teach him how to better use his computer.

Also in 2011, Warren made a deal to acquire Lubrizol, a maker of engine additives, for $9.7 billion. Warren's heir apparent, David Sokol, later resigned from Berkshire Hathaway after it was learned that he had personally bought stock in advance of advising Warren to buy the company.

Warren announced in early 2012 that a successor had been selected but declined to identify the individual. He also revealed that he has prostate cancer but expects to make a full recovery. The 81-year-old joked at the annual meeting that he is more likely to die from a jealous husband.

At the conclusion of the writing of this book, Warren Buffett shows little sign of slowing down. Each new acquisition or occasional sale provokes thorough discussion of the latest nuances in his deal-making and investment style.

=== WARREN WAY 71 ===

Match Your People to Your Principles

"I said we would have people to match our principles, rather than the reverse," Buffett once mused. "But I found out that wasn't so easy."

Further Reading

Melanie Billings-Yun, *Beyond Dealmaking: Five Steps to Negotiating Profitable Relationships* (San Francisco: Jossey-Bass, 2010). Filled with real-life examples of negotiations that have gone right and wrong, this book shows the author's view of how fairness, honesty, empathy, flexibility, and mutual problem solving lead to sustainable success. Dr. Billings-Yun has spent the past 20 years assisting international businesses, nongovernmental organizations, and public agencies with negotiations. This book does not include the negotiation strategies of the world's greatest dealmaker, Warren Buffett.

James Pickens, *The Art of Closing Any Deal* (New York: Business Plus, 2003). This book could more accurately be titled "How to Ruthlessly Lie, Manipulate, and Use Mind Games to Make a Sale." It provides a no-holds-barred guide to getting your way—not just in closing a sale, but in everything you do. This exceedingly detailed, candidly written guide to mind control sold more than a million copies. The book uses anecdotes sparingly, but weaves in plenty of examples. It does not contain the deal-making philosophies of Warren Buffett, the man engaged in 70 distinct lines of business.

Lawrence Cunningham, *The Essays of Warren Buffett: Lessons for Corporate America* (Carolina Academic Press, 2001). Experienced readers of Warren Buffett's letters to the shareholders of Berkshire Hathaway Inc. receive valuable information about how to conduct business. These essays distill Buffett's basic principles of sound business practices in plain words. The book is not organized around any central theme, such as deal making.

Alice Schroeder, *The Snowball: Warren Buffett and the Business of Life* (New York: Bantam Books, 2009). This book was number one on the *New York Times* bestseller list. It provides the most comprehensive look into Warren Buffett's life and philosophies that the world is ever likely to see. The book was produced through five years of interviews with Buffett and covers every facet of his life, but it is not organized around topics. It contains no section on closing deals.

Mary Buffett and David Clark, *The Tao of Warren Buffett* (New York: Scribner, 2006). Like the sayings of the ancient Chinese philosopher Lao-tzu, Warren Buffett's worldly Way is deceptively simple and enormously powerful in application. These are the smart, funny, and memorable sayings that reveal the life philosophy and investment strategies that have made Warren Buffett, and the shareholders of Berkshire Hathaway, so enormously wealthy. This book covers a broad spectrum and does not focus on Warren Buffett's approach to closing a deal.

Robert G. Hagstrom, *The Warren Buffett Way* (Hoboken, NJ: John Wiley & Sons, 2005). Originally published in 1994, this book has sold 1.2 million copies. While the book is mostly about investing, it does contain lessons on buying a business and the psychology of money. The book does not look at deal making.

Simon Reynolds, *Thoughts of Chairman Buffett* (New York: Harper-Collins, 1998). This book is a collection of quotations gathered from a variety of sources. Warren Buffett did not participate in compiling these quotations and did not endorse the book. It is a small book of pithy sayings, not an advice book on any topic, including closing a deal.

Janet Lowe, *Warren Buffett Speaks* (Hoboken, NJ: John Wiley & Sons, 2007). A second edition updated to reflect Warren Buffett's life over the previous 10 years, the book contains a collection of quotes, writings, and favorite sayings from the world's most successful investor. Warren Buffett cooperated with the book project, as did his buddy Bill Gates. The quotes are well organized, but there is no section on deal making.

Mary Buffett and David Clark, *Warren Buffett's Management Secrets* (New York: Simon & Schuster 2009). This book provides an in-depth look at Warren Buffett's philosophies for personal and professional management. Mary Buffett, Warren Buffett's ex-daughter-in-law, gained her insights through being married to Warren's son Peter for 12 years. The lessons cover topics like picking a company to work for, delegating, motivating employees, and managerial challenges. There is nothing on deal making.

Notes

1. Ellyn Spragins, "Building a Company Warren Buffett Would Buy," *Fortune Small Business*, February 1, 2003.
2. Jennifer Reingold, "The Ballad of Clayton Homes," *Fast Company*, January 2004.
3. Joseph Calandro, Jr., "Taking Clayton Homes Private," *Journal of Private Equity*, Vol. 13, no. 3, 2010.
4. Barnett C. Helzberg, Jr., *What I Learned Before I Sold to Warren Buffett* (New York: John Wiley & Sons, 2003).
5. Natalie Doss, "Buffett Poised to Win Bet on U.S. with Burlington," Bloomberg News, February 29, 2012.
6. Ibid.
7. Rana Foroohar, "Warren Buffett Is on a Radical Track," *Time*, January 23, 2012.
8. Alice Schroeder, *The Snowball: Warren Buffett and the Business of Life*, (New York: Bantam Books, 2009), p. 424.
9. Alice Schroeder, *The Snowball: Warren Buffett and the Business of Life* (New York: Bantam Books, 2009), p. 458.
10. Anthony Bianco, "The Warren Buffett You Don't Know," *BusinessWeek*, July 5, 1999.
11. David Marcus, "Berkshire Hathaway/Lubrizol," *American Lawyer*, Vol. 33, no. 5, May 2011.

Index

Price:
fair *vs.* wonderful, 169
as one factor among many, 178
value *vs.*, 170
Price negotiation, CEO and, 76
Primary Sourcing, 35–36
Pritzker family, 189
Problems, solving, 11, 39, 58–59
Process maps, 52
Procurement (Purchasing), 19–20
Profits, sharing your, 177
Promises, keeping your, 182
Prospects:
black-hole, 21
focusing on your, 105
in-denial, 122
indifferent, 120–121
involved, 121–122
"other choices" of, 70–71
profiling your, 116–125
training, 52–53
Public relations people, 72

Q
Quality:
certification of, 28
choosing, 172
defining, 41
Question(s):
asking, 129
responding to, 136
starting with a, 77
tough, 144–145

R
RC Willey, xiv, 15–16, 81, 82, 187
Reach, understanding your deal-
making, 170
Reference checking, 134
References, using, 60–61
Research, limitations of, 174
Researching deals, 173
Reserves, setting aside, 177
Reviews, formal, 133
Reynolds, Simon, 206
RFPs, 19
Risk, xiii, 113
big deal makers and, 41, 43

ubiquity of, 174
Risky deals, avoiding, 169
Road map, deal maker's, 166–167
Roadblocks, 12–13
Rohm and Haas, 201
ROI schedule, establishing an, 78
Roles, assigning, 23, 83–84
Rooney, Frank, 37–39
Roosevelt, Franklin, 191
Rosier, Grady, 100
Russell Corp., 188, 200

S
Sabotage, internal, 134
Salomon Brothers, 81, 127, 129, 176,
187, 197
Sanborn Map Company, 194
Scaling issues, 28
Schey, Ralph, 9
Schloss, Walter, 193
Schroeder, Alice, 90, 127, 206
Schur Packaging Systems, 51
Scott Fetzer Companies, xiv, 9–10, 29,
186, 197
Screening deals, 110
Securities and Exchange Commission
(SEC), 153, 196, 201
See, Mary, 139–140
See's Candies, xiv, 139–141, 186, 196
Self-image, your, 165
Sellers of businesses, 175
Senior executives, 34, 75–76
Shaw Industries, 111, 188, 199
Showing up, 176
Simplicity, seeking, 45, 133, 174
Simpson, Lou, 200
Slippery slope, 157
The Snowball (Alice Schroeder), xiii,
176, 177, 206
Sokol, David, 153–154, 189, 203
Solution, finding your, 103–104
Spitzer, Eliot, 199
Splitting the pie, 108
Spragins, Ellyn, 32
Star Furniture, 81–82
Starting from where you are, 29
Steps, outlining the, 77
Strategic Resource Group, 100

About the Authors

TOM SEARCY has established himself as the foremost expert in large account sales. As an author, speaker, consultant, and founder of Hunt Big Sales, Tom has helped his clients generate business in excess of $5 billion. Leading four companies through tremendous growth of less than $15 million to over $100 million in each case, Tom perfected the process for consistently landing large accounts. This process is documented in his books, *Whale Hunting: How to Land Big Sales and Transform Your Company* and *RFPs Suck! How to Master the RFP System Once and for All to Win Big Business*. Searcy writes online weekly columns for Forbes, Inc. and CBS' *MoneyWatch*, which have a combined monthly readership of 38 million. Searcy's expertise has been quoted in *The Wall Street Journal, Financial Times UK,* and *Inc. Magazine.*

HENRY J. DEVRIES is an educator, columnist, and author who speaks to thousands of business owners and executives each year. He teaches marketing and is the assistant dean of continuing education at the University of California

San Diego. A former president of a large West Coast advertising and public relations agency, he helped the firm double revenues and earn a spot in the Ad Age 500 by closing deals with companies like Marriott, PETCO, and Sunkist. Henry is a columnist for *U-T San Diego* and Forbes.com, a TV commentator, and the coauthor of *Self-Marketing Secrets, Pain Killer Marketing,* and *Closing America's Job Gap.* He earned his MBA at San Diego State University and has completed certificate programs at the Harvard Business School.